I'm in Search of *Myself*...

Have You Seen Me Anywhere?

Patty Kasian

Copyright © 2020 Patty Kasian
All rights reserved
First Edition

NEWMAN SPRINGS PUBLISHING
320 Broad Street
Red Bank, NJ 07701

First originally published by Newman Springs Publishing 2020

ISBN 978-1-64801-974-6 (Paperback)
ISBN 978-1-64801-975-3 (Digital)

Printed in the United States of America

To all my fellow kindred spirits.

Introduction

WE ARE BORN INTO THIS physical body to attend earth school. Sometimes the classes we have chosen to take seemed filled with uncertainty, and the next moment, they're deliriously joyful. We spend a great deal of time trying to find out who we are, where we belong, and how we fit in. We search and wander around and make plans for our lives and our futures, but at the same time, life just happens.

A while back, a friend was facilitating an exciting workshop designed to help the group uncover what they really believed in, to discover their purpose in life, and to make their lives more passionate. I think God must have invented "passion," to teach us how to fly!

I believe in divine guidance and that serendipity or coincidences are available to us all the time, we just need to pay attention. It's like when we are in the right place at the perfect time or open a book to the exact page for the question that was on our mind.

Maybe it's when we think of a long lost friend and surprisingly, they call. It's all a matter of listening.

I've had innumerable amazing, funny, and unexplainable experiences and people have asked me for years to gather these stories together and share them. The words "I'm in search of myself, have you seen me anywhere" seemed amusingly appropriate.

So now, I am sharing my inspirational, serious and humorous, astonishing, and very spiritual journey with you. Each chapter relates to something different and may bring up more feelings or ideas than you expected, and you might have new questions to your old answers. I hope you laugh as often as I did and live life passionately, even on the darkest, or most glorious days, that visit us all.

This book is filled with true experiences I've had in my life. Each chapter shares a separate situation or emotion. It covers life and death, love and passion, kids, courage, trust and forgiveness, hope and faith, and just plain silliness.

I have been watched over on this journey, in ways I can't even explain and have often thought God and my guardian angels must be working overtime, on me!

I feel we need to live life purposefully, every day. We need to radiate our love to everyone and be filled with faith and joy and kindness. We need to be authentic and true to ourselves and live and love and laugh equally.

I believe we are all where we are supposed to be when we get there. So get comfy and enjoy the ride. Life is a participation sport!

Chapter 1

MY LIFE HAS BEEN LIKE skipping stones, with new beginnings all the time, and no idea where the ripples would take me. Once again, I was headed out on another ambiguous journey.

The year had flown by and it was Christmas time already. I was heading out on a road trip with my two children to my sister's house in Utah. The weather was perfect. It was one of those soft, feathery snow days I liked so much. I had made this trip to my sister's house many times for the holiday festivities and vacations and she always wanted us to move there. I loved the area for many reasons, but also enjoyed returning home to California. Then that fall, to everyone's surprise, I actually moved to Utah. But that time, the reason was different. I had a mysterious purpose that kept me there.

Mary and I were separated when we were young and never had the chance to be close. Well, there was that time she lived with me during her college summer break, and we drove each other nuts, but that doesn't really count. We didn't get reacquainted until after high school. I missed not having an older sister available.

The memories of the past swirled through my head, as I neared her child-filled home. I called them just before I left my house and her kids seemed to plot my exact route and expected time of arrival. They took into consideration how many times we stopped at tourist spots and how long the pit stops could possibly be and would be waiting out front on the porch or down on the corner just as we arrived. How did they do that? Each one of them was bubbling over with enthusiasm and had to catch me up on every detail since our last visit.

Mary's house was the gathering place for the holidays. She lived for the days when the whole family could be together. The adult children popped in and brought their friends and in moments, the house was brimming with the Christmas spirit. Her friends and neighbors might stop over and she grabbed another plate for any additional guest.

I brought special treats and the things I called fun foods, were luxuries for her family of ten children. As a surprise, I put the eggnog, cheese, and eggs in her milk box on the porch. She went outside to check if the milk had arrived and lit up with glee.

"Look what the milkman left us for Christmas!" We all laughed because it never occurred to her that someone other than the milkman brought her dairy goodies. What a silly girl. It was hard to resist teasing her, since she was so gullible.

I was staying in a motel and Mary called early in the morning and asked, "When will you be here? The kids are getting restless and want to open presents."

I could hear them in the background. Her house was filled with more chaotic activity than I was used to and so the morning drive was worth the extra moments of peace and quiet.

One of my nieces spent the night with me and helped me load the car with gifts. I scraped the snow from the windows and left the car running by the curb to warm up for the short but chilly drive. I juggled the presents as I locked the door to the house, when I heard the car door being slammed shut, locking my keys inside the car.

I was partially comforted when my niece smiled hesitantly and said, "Well, at least your car won't be stolen, since your keys are locked safely—inside the car."

I enjoyed the many road trips and vacations with my two young children. It was the three of us for many years and it seemed that traveling kept us connected because as we drove, we were all a captive audience. I never had an equal partner who shared my gusto for life and adventure, so whenever I had time off from work, I packed up the kids in my four-wheel-drive truck and we hit the road. I figured life needed to be lived, not viewed, even if it meant going alone since my husband always chose to stay home.

I packed lots of books and toys and music. We played license plate games, and I spy. I even had earmuffs, not so much in anticipation of the cold and delightful snow, but I think it was to save me from hearing, "One million bottles of pop on the wall" or "The Sound of Music" again and again. I caught on after a while that it was them who needed a reprieve from my singing. You know it's bad when your girl's glee teacher suggests you might want to take another elective class. A recently married friend of mine just returned from his first vacation as a new parent of two youngsters.

He asked me, "Do you know how many times they can sing that song on a trip?"

I laughed and said, "I do know that answer!"

I was the middle child and always had quite a spunky spirit. My younger brother followed me like a little puppy dog and would do anything I asked. I would be doubled over in laughter as the goat and geese chased after him, trying to bite his backside and grab the snacks I intentionally snuck into his pockets.

"Maybe you should get in the rabbit hutch, Robbie, where you'll be safe. Come here, I'll give you a boost."

At dinnertime, my mom would ask, "Where is your brother?" suspecting that I would know where he was, since we got into everything together.

"Oops, I think he got in the rabbit hutch again!"

Then there was the time our dad took us hiking in the mountains and we came upon a small hill.

I told Robbie, "Let's have a race to the bottom, you jump off this hill and I'll roll down and see who gets there first."

Surprisingly, as a kid, he never had broken bones or stitches, unlike me, but did have to have his stomach pumped when he tried a suspicious dog treat I found. Mary rarely participated in our foolishness.

What a blessing siblings are—in retrospect. Mary, Robbie, and I were very close in age, but as different as the sun, and the moon, and the stars.

The idea of living in Utah was so unexpected. I had one of those years that I wished I had gallons of Wite-Out to erase oodles of life's little practical jokes. So moving to Utah came as a bigger surprise to me than to my relatives.

I had been feeling the need for change for some time and so it was easy for me to leave Los Angeles and accept the job offer in Northern Montana, one of the most picturesque places on the planet. My daughter Jeni would join me after graduation from high school in June, and we would drive back to our new home. After several negotiations, I was finally hired and I quickly packed and left my friends and comfort zone behind to start the spring season off with a brand new, interesting job.

Any sense of fear or doubt I may have had at starting a new venture in unfamiliar territory was rapidly replaced with a sense of excitement and expectation for a better way of life.

The job was delayed for a month, so I decided to explore the country for a bit.

My dad would tease me, "You must be part gypsy the way you can travel on a dime."

He was an armchair traveler and found pleasure in making road maps for me. He drew very well, so the maps almost looked official, with legend and highway signs and tourist trivia spots. He added interesting tidbits about certain locations, knowing I would check it out. I loved to meander and sightsee and visit the biggest barn or rocking chair. I followed the Lewis and Clark trail, stopped by John Wayne's childhood house, crossed through the covered bridges of Madison County, and went by to check on Francesca and Robert Kincaid's place. I went to "Field of Dreams" movie site. And yes, as I sat on the bleachers, the energy felt so alive, I really believed the ball players would be coming out of the corn stalks to play ball!

My dad was enthusiastic to hear the stories upon my return.

I was so logical that my friends and family couldn't believe I was running off willy-nilly to chase some illusive dream. I felt this move would change my life. I was once again, daring to step out and take a chance. It seemed I had been in charge of myself since I was young and was miraculously protected and blessed along the way and had to believe this was still the case, so the choice was easy.

I was anxious for Jeni to arrive. I wanted to show her all the incredible scenery. Being a city kid, I thought she would like this small town and our cabin by the lake. I was breathless by such beauty. I closed my eyes and could envision the gently flowing rivers with the fly fishermen casting their poles like a magic wand. The lines would gracefully drift through the air, like a feather tossed gently in the breeze and land in a precise location on the water. The azure lakes were sparkling and when looking at a photograph, you couldn't tell where the majestic mountains began and the deep mirrored water ended.

Friends would say, "How can you move to Montana? You breathe air you can't even see, *and* everyone waves at you with a full, open hand!"

Jeni's graduation day finally arrived. I had so many mixed emotions about my graduation and all the memories that crept out.

Both of my children were out of the nest and on their way to adulthood. I was so grateful to finally be free of the rocky times that remarried spouses stirred into my mulligan stew pot of life.

When Jeni arrived to her new state, we took a driving trip and traveled as far as we could in one day to experience the glorious country. I wanted her to be in awe, just as I was and appreciate this natural, smogless beauty that was free to behold.

It seemed like we had been driving for hours and the miles went unnoticed, when we found ourselves at the Canadian border. We stopped at the checkpoint and waited. There didn't appear to be anyone there, which seemed unusual.

She was skeptical when I said, "I guess we can just drive into Canada." We crossed over the border and continued on.

Immediately, alarms went off and this booming voice bellowed out over the loud speaker, "Turn around, RIGHT NOW!"

Holy smokes, will we be arrested? I swiftly turned my truck around like a stunt driver in an action movie. We listened intently as the intimidating guard lectured us, and we assured him we weren't sneaking into his country and would never cross the border again, without permission. We drove off and looked at each other and started to laugh.

Jeni remarked, "Just another ordinary day out with you, Mom!"

I loved Montana and felt it was the right place, but possibly the wrong time, as things went from bad to worse. I quickly discovered that my dream job was, in reality, a nightmare. My paychecks were bouncing on a regular basis.

The employer responded, "What's the big deal, you get paid, eventually."

That was certainly not the answer I expected. I went to the bank to explain what was going on, since the numerous checks I had written were suddenly useless. While I was there, another check was returned and I couldn't believe it. That paycheck was two weeks old, how could it bounce? I sat there and began to cry.

My finances were in serious jeopardy. What else could possibly go wrong? I used up my savings and couldn't replace the checks. The lender of my leased car called, and I tried to tell him the story about my employer's checks, but that next day, I looked out my office window, just in time to see my car being repoed away.

I found a second job to stay afloat. It paid $5 an hour and all I had to do was answer the phones. The thoughtful employee before my shift left a small vase of home-grown flowers next to the phone console.

I worked around office equipment long enough to know the vase shouldn't be there and thought about moving the flowers. In that instant, before I even touched it, the wobbly vase tipped over and emptied the water into the computer phone system, which immediately shut down all the phones throughout the resort, who was hosting several conferences. It wasn't a pretty sight, and even harder to explain, "Really, I didn't do it." I enjoyed the job while it lasted.

Then, Jeni decided to move back to California. She said, "There is nothing to do here."

She couldn't find a job or meet new friends and college wouldn't start for a couple of months. She missed her friends and two young half-brothers.

What sealed the deal for her was when she almost mowed down a deer that leaped in front of her car and ran her off the road.

She was ready to go back home. "LA doesn't have livestock on the streets."

She didn't think it was funny when I remarked, "Oh *deer*!"

I was *so* lonely and things continued to spiral out of my control, as if I was in a deep, black hole.

The good news was that I was now, by mutual agreement, unemployed, or in other words, fired.

The boss stated, "The reason being, you could not organize the office and get the business started as you promised by your experience."

I was angry to hear that answer and snapped back, "You can certainly fire me for any reason, but not for disorganization. I can organize anything and have proven that on bigger projects than this, and was paid for it."

They did change the terminology, and of course, I wasn't let go because of my organizational skills or "reversal pay" and my bad attitude toward that. So I guess being unemployed was one less worry for me, as I started my new job at the convenience store.

I wondered what this experience taught me. I came all this way just to lose everything I was attached to. Simplicity—what a true wonder.

I couldn't find an appropriate job and figured it was time to leave my Montana dream behind and move on, but what would I do? Where would I go? Everything I now owned fit in my car.

I realized one of the most important things I lost was my happy, positive sense of self. I was defeated. I definitely needed an attitude adjustment to go along with my relocation and job search. What had I done in the past?

I decided to make *that* moving day a new year, and with that came resolutions. This would be my new and improved year. I casually checked out my horoscope and it stated, "An inspirational message will bring a new slant on an old reality. You will inherit peace and calm." It seemed I should look up the meaning of those words, peace and calm, since they sounded so foreign. I read on, "Your efforts will be rewarded in many ways. Take time to be still—in the stillness, you shall know me." I guess the search for *me* was just beginning.

My resolutions were, I will remember to be grateful, for something, every day. I will have an "attitude of gratitude." Since I seemed to be on a roll of self-improvement ideas, I added more. I will listen to my inner guidance and trust the answers. I will be loving and kind and not so critical, especially of myself. I will be the best I can be and let go of any old fears and resentments. Let me find and keep love, as well as give it away, unconditionally. I will "let go and Let God."

I added, sometimes I worry unnecessarily, so hang on to me, God, and help me keep my faith and find the smile in my heart, again. I will be patient and allow people to be who they are and respect everyone for their differences. I will radiate love to everyone I meet and most importantly, I will remember this throughout the whole year, staring today. I was making a serious commitment and it made me misty-eyed as I wrote it down, because it felt so real. I like to write things down for clarity.

When I left Montana, I had planned to visit Mary and stay for a couple of weeks and then be on my way again. Maybe I could find a job in Colorado. One niece and her family lived outside of Denver and one nephew was working in Denver, and maybe I could get a job with his employer. Andy always was on the lookout for anything I was on the lookout for.

"I can mention you to my boss, he is looking for someone who does what you do."

I had a different relationship with each one of Mary's kids, and we always helped each other in various ways.

Two weeks came and went, and my car was packed, and I was ready to leave Utah, when I had quite the extraordinary experience.

I was making one last restroom stop before I got on the road and checking my hair in the mirror. My dad had passed on a few years back, and just before he died, we had unpleasant words and we didn't speak again. We never argued, probably from lack of desire or opportunity, so this was very unusual. As I look back, it seemed he was intentionally trying to pick a fight with me, maybe to justify his lack of parenting or taking responsibility for his choices that negatively affected our family. I let him off the hook a lot over the years, but on that day, as he kept provoking me, I would make him accountable.

Shortly after that argument with my dad, my stepmom called. She demanded to know what happened.

"What did you say to your dad? Whatever it was, it's making him sicker. His emphysema is getting worse and he can barely breathe. You've got to call him and apologize, he's going to die."

I told her, "This is between the two of us, I would take back anything that wasn't true, but I meant what I said and he knows it *is* true and that's all there is."

He never told her what our "private" fight was about.

I had a different kind of bond with my dad, even under the circumstances of not being raised by him. I was always the kid in tow, always wanting another story, another adventure from him. Mary and Robbie were never interested. I reminded him so much of my mom, his wife Janet, who he adored more than anything. He was proud of who I became, as I made my own way into adulthood. I stood up for myself, and for the underdog, provided for my children, functioned well in the business world, and lived life fully. I had that same spark and smile and passion that she had.

When I took up flying and realized how expensive lessons were, I joined Civil Air Patrol. That was the answer. I could learn to fly, do search and rescues, be a cadet leader, work in fundraising. I was happy!

My dad's reaction surprised me; he was beaming. "Your mom was in Civil Air Patrol also!"

He went to the other room and came back with a picture of her wearing her Civil Air Patrol uniform and gave it to me. What a precious gift.

He asked me, "When I die, will you take my ashes up in the plane and scatter them over my favorite hiking mountain?"

That idea reminded him of how he enjoyed nature, camping, and hiking, artificial leg and all, and so I did. My main worry was that he would come back *in* the plane! That would be my goodbye, until we met again.

My stepmom made me promise to do the same with her ashes, at the same spot. When she died, my stepsister called to give me the news and remind me of that promise.

"Where exactly on the mountain is Dad?" she asked.

I had to laugh. "Since I threw him out of a plane, he's *all* over the mountain!"

I was making one last restroom stop at the gas station before I got on the road and was checking my hair and makeup in the mirror. But in that moment, as I stood there in front of the mirror, I saw the sight of my dad's face and I heard his voice. I blinked my eyes and looked around the room. Was there anyone to witness this? To my surprise, I wasn't afraid.

He said to me, "You have to stay here and take care of you sister." I was stunned. I expected if I ever did "feel" his spirit or "hear" a message, he would tell me how much he loved me and how sorry he was for what he did.

A couple of days after he died, I was at their house and slept in his bed due to the full house and lack of other options. I seemed to have a connection to the spirit world, especially in dreams. If someone has passed, they come back to talk or comfort me. It's not like seeing ghosts or hearing voices, but a feeling and a knowing and wasn't I scared about bad vibes or whatever. He never came, I never felt his presence. Of course, the moment the heater kicked on abruptly in the middle of the night and shook their mobile home, I shot out of that bed like an arrow and ran down the hall!

His message was clear. My dad knew Mary was facing an extremely rough road ahead and he also knew I was strong enough to lead the way for her, not financially, but by example. I wondered how I was supposed to help her? What did he mean? What could possibly happen to her, or her children? He knew I would listen and without hesitation, I would stay and do what I could. I felt, this must be really serious, if that was the *only* message he needed to tell me.

I thought, I don't have a job or a place to live, so if this message is real and I find a job and a house, *now*, I will stay in Utah. As a test, I would check one newspaper, that's all. Being Sunday, I thought I would be back on my way in no time. The paper I checked was one of those free papers at the gas station.

I called the number and the lady named Bev responded, "Can you come over now?"

We hit it off right away and I told her, "I am unemployed, but expect to find work very soon."

She welcomed me into her home and said, "You can rent the downstairs apartment and pay the balance of the rent in a week."

I was amazed how this was coming together. I unpacked my car and drove back to Mary's house, just a short distance away.

She was puzzled and asked, "What did you forget?"

I answered, "You won't believe this, but I am staying in Utah. I found a place to live and can look for work tomorrow."

She giggled with delight and said, "Wow, what a great surprise!"

Mary's friend, Sammie, popped in for a quick visit and said, "I can take you job-hunting tomorrow." I felt the right and perfect job would just show up because of all these unexpected turn of events.

He took me to the local college, and I found an ad for a company that had three positions available, and I was qualified for any one of them. I faxed my resume and the secretary called me back in a few minutes.

She said, "The boss may have a different job for you, can you come in now?"

A different job, what does that mean?

This was another one of those unexplainable things that sure felt like a miracle. I asked for a house and a job, and there they were. I was testing my faith and was pleasantly surprised when I found exactly what I ordered. I didn't tell Mary then about my experience with Dad because she probably wouldn't have understood or believed it anyway, but in time, she would.

So I waited to learn why I needed to stay in Utah, and how I could help Mary and her family, and especially, what my dad's urgent message meant.

Chapter 2

IT SEEMS THAT JOBS ALWAYS find me. Years ago, I worked in a coffee shop and a doctor's wife and their medical assistant, Sharon, came in every day for lunch. They loved my cheery attitude and mentioned I should come by and meet the doctor. After work, I ran errands and wandered around and eventually popped in about five.

Sharon seemed annoyed, "Where have you been?"

I was puzzled, "What do you mean, you said just drop by and here I am."

She replied, "This is a job interview."

I was surprised and responded, "Oh, really?"

I was hired on the spot and was trained for front office and then shortly afterward, trained for back office because I was good with the patients.

My first summer job in high school was working in a factory, making doorknobs on an assembly line. I was young and fast and efficient and had to wait for other workers to complete their tasks before I could do my job, and it gave me too much free time. I was working a waitress job also because I was saving up to buy a car, so I would go wait in the bathroom lounge area and would fall asleep.

The boss decided he better give me work somewhere else, so I wouldn't be dependent on others timing, or nap on the job! He had a special project with a deadline. He thought I could assist that team and get the order delivered faster. Come to find out, I got the order done faster than two shifts of workers. So he gave me another job as relief PBX operator.

When that job was done, he said, "I don't know what to do with you. Can you go into the office and match up receipts?"

That was the end of factory work; accounting, here I come!

Then there was the job at the finance company. The company I worked for was relocating to San Francisco and we could all go with them or they would try to find us jobs. They lined up interviews and staggered them throughout the week and sent us out in groups of two. My co-worker Tony and I were the first to go and I drove. Our meeting was set for 8:00 AM. We were very close to the company, but I couldn't find the street because of construction in the area. I called them and they gave directions. It was now eight thirty, and we were still lost. Tony was getting stressed as I called them again, and they gave me better directions.

The road kept looping with dead ends, and I still couldn't find it. It was nine o'clock, and the building was nowhere in sight.

Tony snapped, "Does that sign say San Diego?"

He was about to choke me, since he needed that job.

He advised me, "We need to reschedule, this is so bad. We look like idiots."

I called once again, "I am so sorry, but I can't get to your street."

They patiently gave me clear, specific instructions.

Tony was getting real upset.

He hollered, "Let's go back to our office, this is ridiculous!"

"We can't go back and say we couldn't even find the building. We need to be able to give everyone the right directions."

He paused, "Okay, but then we are going back."

It was ten o'clock, and we finally found the way to the street and then the building was visible.

I don't know what I was thinking when I remarked, "Since we are here anyway, we might as well go in and apologize and hopefully reschedule our interviews."

He was beside himself and declared, "I'm not going in there." He was angry and had no intention of speaking with anyone.

"Oh, come on, we are here, they will understand because the street was hard to find with all the construction and detours."

He had to make a pit stop, so he went in the building with me. I was prepared and I wanted this job and was going to leave my resume anyway.

We got into the elevator, looked at each other, and began to laugh. What a crazy ordeal. He went into the restroom, and I went into the supervisor's office.

I started to apologize, "So sorry…"

But as I was trying to explain, I started laughing. It was all over, I just laid my resume on his desk and turned and walked out. I was called back for a second interview and I was the only one hired!

The boss said, "Now remember, we start work at eight o'clock!"

I might be having a similar experience with this potential employer. He was out of town and received a copy of my fax from his secretary.

He told the secretary, "Get her in today."

I thought, *Well, this is interesting.* They advertised three different positions, but had something else in mind for me. What could that possibly be?

I agreed to meet with his wife beforehand and meet with him when he returned. The interview was for the position as his personal assistant, working out of his home and not in the office. I wasn't sure how I felt about that. It seemed unusual, and then I smiled as I thought, *But for me, maybe not!* The most amazing jobs have always found me!

I was impressed with my new potential boss. He was a prominent businessman in the city and was involved in many huge projects. He needed someone to organize his office, monitor his rental properties, oversee construction, do in-depth accounting and record keeping, and generally keep him together. This was the job for me, since I was born to organize.

I wasn't familiar with the area and drove by the house before the interview, so there would be no problem with finding the place at the scheduled time. My niece came along, since this interview was sort of odd. Oh my, I looked backed down at my notes to double-check the address. I had pulled up in front of a mansion. He was a millionaire and lived in a mansion! No one would believe this. I went in later for the interview and listened as he described what the job would entail and was confident when he asked, "And why should I hire you?"

I looked around the room at a huge disorganized mess, with papers and overstuffed boxes everywhere.

I grinned and said, "I can definitely fix this!"

He exclaimed, "When can you start?"

This job would be a new experience. I was very methodical and when everyone else was scattered, I was calm and in control. Ben gave me opportunities to utilize every talent I had, and even those I didn't know I had.

He had offices all over, and I was talking to one of his secretaries. She told me, "I like you."

I accepted the compliment, but I guess I looked puzzled. "Why?"

She replied, "You are the first person I've seen that has kept Ben organized and made it look easy."

Other employees were intimidated by him because the work was always needed—yesterday.

He was a tenacious businessman with unique ideas, and I was becoming proficient in making this job flow easily and effortlessly. He asked if I could do this project or that task, and sometimes I didn't know because I never did it before, but I always replied, "I'll try, and if I can do it, great, and if I can't, then at least we'll know."

He liked my attitude.

I finally got to meet his daughter, Vivian. She was beautiful and very talented and involved in beauty pageants. She came into my office to chat, which was not a routine event, but a welcome surprise.

She said, "My parents talk about you all the time and how everything is under control and you always have or can get the answers. They say you are doing a good job and you're the best assistant he's ever had."

I was almost embarrassed by her kind words. But it was true; Ben went from project to project, and I would be interacting with everyone involved and would have reports and financial statistics ready almost before he asked and information available just as he needed it. He was everywhere and involved in everything, and I kept up with his rigorous ventures and welcomed the challenges. I even amazed myself sometimes!

Vivian had entered another beauty contest, and she had a rigid daily itinerary. I read through it and noticed she didn't have any fun in her full day. How can you have life without fun? She had coaches and classes for everything. Her whole day was planned to the last minute.

I shared my opinion, "Something is missing here."

Ben inquired, "Can you help her have fun with all of this?"

He decided to make me her "attitude" coach.

I started with, "First thing in the morning, you get up and look at yourself in the mirror, even without makeup, and give yourself a mental hug and silently shout to yourself, or out loud if you choose, GOOD MORNING, I LOVE YOU! And I will love *you*, all this day. Say it with such conviction that every fiber of your being knows it's true. Use positive affirmations during the day and while you exercise, giggle. Then take a nurturing, soothing bath at night. Laugh out loud. Visualize the desired outcome. Feel it, as if it's already so."

I stood in front of a podium and instructed her to focus and just be herself. I saw her dad in the corner of my eye as he passed by his den office. He would walk back and forth listening to my words, but letting me continue without interruption. I wasn't going to say anything I didn't believe, and there was no sugar coating because of who she was. She listened attentively, and I could see the sparkle in her eyes grow with each new suggestion.

I acknowledged, "Sure, this is an important pageant, but you need to be the best you can be, inside as well as out."

She had won and lost pageants before. I told her, "This inner beauty, confidence, and self-esteem that is your foundation for today, can be used in every aspect of your life, every day."

She was amazed by my words, as if what I was saying was a brand new concept.

I said, "It's not selfish to love yourself, I think it's a necessity of survival."

She listened and paused before she asked her question, "Do you love yourself?"

My answer came quickly, "Yes, indeed I do!" (Even without makeup!)

Vivian took voice lessons in New York and when she was in town, her operatic voice resonated throughout the house as she practiced, and in time she had the voice of an angel. She played the harp and that only added to the vision. Ben was filled with pride as he listened to his youngest daughter rehearse for a variety of performances.

The pageant was over and Ben asked me, "Do you know what I would like to do?"

"What?"

New ideas were always bouncing around in his head and it could have been anything.

"I want to create an opera company for the state of Utah, can you help to organize this?"

I didn't know much about opera, but answered, "Sure, I can organize anything and can learn about opera as I go."

We started this gigantic project, *Utah Lyric Opera Society*. We brought in amazing talent from all over Utah. Their voices were incredible, and it brought tears to my eyes as the sweet tones and harmonies kept replaying in my ears, even after they were done rehearsing.

The first performance was *La Boheme*, and we had a formal dinner for over five hundred people and brought in an opera star from the New York Met who dazzled the audience. Everything went off without a hitch, as if by magic.

There were several performances throughout the year and I was involved in organizing and coordinating all aspects of the sold-out opera seasons. What a tremendous experience.

We had romantic operas on Valentine's Day and comedies in the summer and heartwarming performances in the winter. I was getting to know the patrons by sight and would greet them personally, by name, at each opera.

Ben was regularly surprised at the magical influence I had on the opera guests. They looked forward to the new season's calendar, and I enjoyed seeing them again. I loved dressing up in formal attire and watching the operas unfold successfully each time.

Vivian's marriage proposal came after one of the performances on Valentine's Day. The wedding dinner and reception was held at Ben's home and was extravagant, and so elegant. The elaborate decorations thrilled the many guests, as the line of well-wishers stretched down the block for hours, to greet the charming new couple.

I told my friends, "If I had never had a job before, I could now do anything because of the faith Ben had in me and the opportunities he gave me."

Whenever he had a new idea and asked, "Can you do this?" I never knew the word "no" or "I can't." I always knew the answer would come, by trying.

Ben enjoyed the sound of children laughing and playing around the house. One of his three grown children brought his grandchildren by every day.

Their beautiful and loving home was the hub of continuous business, family and entertaining. The gently winding staircase with elegance cherry wood handrails led up to my office on the second floor. Expensive art decorated the walls and the room had comfortable velvet couches to go along with the professional office furniture. The lace curtains adorned the glass on my office French doors which opened to expose the landing above the rich forest green marbled foyer. The high ceiling displayed an enormous, but delicate crystal chandelier. When it snowed, the reflection of gentle rays made the room sparkle like brilliant diamonds being tossed around in the air.

Some days I would pick up three of Mary's boys after school and they would come over to my office and hang out until I was ready to go home. The kids enjoyed shoveling snow that had gathered on the gigantic trampoline, buried in the backyard. A snow fight always ensued! I noticed Ben watching out the window and smiling. He was such a generous man. He would pay them to rake the large yard or shovel the snow. They did every chore with such enthusiasm and were always eager to volunteer just to have some spending money.

Whenever I called and asked if they were interested, they immediately shouted, "Yes!"

Their reward, besides money, was when they were done, they got to go to the third level of the house and play video games. They never saw real video games in someone's house before, and, they could play for free. The room resembled an arcade. They could romp and laugh and the rule was always to be respectful of other people's space and property. They always observed my impartial rules and I appreciated that. If they came over to work, they did that first, if they had homework, they did that first, if they had dessert, they ate that first. Just checking to see if you were listening!

I wore many hats while working for Ben. Whether it was supervising, driving, shopping, accounting, opera, or handling many other situations, I always felt very accomplished. I oversaw construction budgets and timeframes on new and rental properties that he planned to repair or sell. He owned several homes and some were being renovated, but the vacant ones created a security risk.

I was still renting at Bev's house when Ben asked, "Would you like to housesit while the repairs are being done on the vacant home?"

"Sure." I didn't mind that idea of living there while they fixed it up.

This particular house was vacant and on the sales market for a year, so I planned on living there for a while. I surveyed the property and visualized the location for planting flowers and where the furniture would go, while each room was under construction. Within one week of moving in, the house sold. Ben couldn't believe it and liked those odds and asked if I wanted to go to another house. This unlikely scenario was becoming quite comical.

I was flexible enough to go with the flow of quick change and had nothing to tie me down to one area. I drove one of their cars, so I could work in the office or travel to other locations, while I continued to do my required duties.

Ben owned a small house, only five thousand square feet, in an upscale neighborhood. It was a luxury home but was a few feet short of being labeled that. It recently became vacant and he wanted everything remodeled and more space added, and this house definitely couldn't be left unattended.

He inquired, "Do you want to camp out there for a while?"

I had seen all of his other properties, except this one. He started to describe the house.

"This is a spacious, luxury home and we lived in it years ago, and it has a lot of sentimental value. It is set back off the road on a private driveway."

It had a secluded area behind the house that was perfect for family and friends gathering for any occasion. It had its own creek that formed the property line.

He continued, "The backyard has two large decks and the gazebo rests on the edge of the creek. The gardener tends to the variety of trees and keeps the lawn and shrubs in order." He described every feature with pride and then waited for my response. He was puzzled because I didn't seem impressed.

He added, "You don't understand, this is an expensive, luxury home."

But all I heard was, "It has a creek and gazebo and trees," and the magic word, "a gardener!" I checked out the backyard long before I ever saw the inside and would have been satisfied staying in a tiny tent in the magnificent backyard.

He said, "You can live here rent free, for as long as it takes to complete the renovations. You will be responsible for the utilities and overseeing the construction."

I couldn't wait to move in. He expected this to be a short stay, but his costly ideas, turned it into a major project, and a couple of weeks turned into a couple of years. In the end, it was never renovated. What an incredible unforeseen blessing for me.

Whenever my friends came over, they were certainly surprised because the directions seemed so rustic.

"Just go down the winding alley, pass over the small bridge, go around the tree that is in the road and then through the gate."

The first personal thing I hung up was my affirmation collage. I am a firm believer in prayer, affirmations, and visualization. I believe all it takes, is a thought, to get a plan into action.

"To *see* is to *be* is my philosophy!"

Norman Vincent Peale said, "Prayerize, picturize, actualize."

I was intrigued many years ago by the book *Creative Visualization* by Shakti Gawain, about visualization to manifest what you desired for your highest good. It got me to pondering the potential and I thought I just might try out that theory. It sounded easy enough and seemed painless.

So I assembled an array of "subliminal" images inside a picture frame. I added pictures of things I wanted, or liked, and expected they would manifest for me, for my highest good, without having to doubt or worry about any of it. I wasn't attached to any rigid game plan and the pictures could be rearranged and revised as my dreams changed or expanded.

So when guests came over and took the house tour and asked me, "How did you ever get to live in a house like *this*?"

I directed them to the top of the stairs where my artwork hung and said, "See that big house in the picture?"

The worn frame contained a picture of a beautiful mansion, five of the most unique, white stretch limos, driving in a row (not going to an awards ceremony) a sailboat and beaches for travel, a seagull for freedom, the first plane I flew when I was taking lessons, a lottery ticket (never can tell about that one) a dollar bill and a book cover. (You have to guess where that one is going!) I didn't need to focus daily, but as I passed by and glanced occasionally, it always had made me smile, because little by little, these things just "showed up."

It's like pizza: if you don't call in your order, it doesn't get delivered to you!

Chapter 3

ANOTHER NEW YEAR—I WRITE AFFIRMATIONS for each new year depending on what I want to accomplish or what had inspired me, and they change as my life changes. Last year my life was happening in full force, and it was like a runaway train. It was emotionally filled to capacity with a broken relationship, my son was in a serious accident, hospitals were trying to sue me, my car was stolen, bills that seemed insurmountable, and a death in the family. It was one of those cycles of life and there wasn't anything I could do, but hang on and just go "through" it. Nothing made any sense and it just kept coming.

I was at my wit's end and my dad sent me a cartoon strip to cheer me up (since we were both related to "Murphy")—a man was resting in his backyard and a huge tennis shoe fell from the sky and smashed his roof. He stood there with his mouth hanging open, staring at the damage, in total disbelief. His wife calmly said, "Should we call the insurance company now, or wait for the other shoe to drop?"

I usually tried to remain optimistic, but at that time, I needed a diversion. I didn't drink or smoke or take drugs. In high school, I knew kids who took drugs and their lives took a serious tumble and I chose not to do that. I always believed I needed to be at peace on the inside first, so I could handle things on the outside, easier. Of course, that was always easier said than done.

I made myself an *affirmation* tape. It wasn't too long or too short and covered all kinds of things. I made it a half an hour long so it would be like a walk in the park, and I listened to it every day.

I magically found things to be different, my attitude was changing, and my problems seemed to come with solutions.

Here are a few of the things I said on the tape to myself, as myself, and to this very day, it still works. If I am in a slump, I listen to the tape and I feel better in no time.

Good morning, thank you for this brand new day and for the many blessings and miracles this day will bring to me.

I know that I am loved.

I love myself and I love all my friends.

I let go of the past and move on with a smile.

I give myself permission to feel my feelings.

I acknowledge any negative feelings and let them go.

I can choose again. (I love this one!)

I am empowered to know and express myself honestly.

I am a child of God and I deserve to be loved.

It's okay for me to be happy and I am.

I am trusting, healthy, wealthy, and wise.

I am entitled to undo any old beliefs, that no longer serve my highest purpose and release them.

I am attracting right relationships into my life. I am allowed forgive myself and others.

I will feed my mind, body, and spirit with positive nutrition.

I can release the junk in the trunk.

I have a positive attitude and laughter in my heart.

Divine guidance is working through me here and now.

I have infinite creative powers.

My higher self is guiding me in everything I do.

The universe is unfolding perfectly.

I don't have to hang on, I can relax and let go.

I can go with the flow.

I have everything I need to enjoy my here and now.

I have all the love I need within my own heart. I am a loveable and loving person.

I am whole in myself.

I am playful and filled with joy.

I am kind and compassionate.

I am willing to be happy.
Every day, I am getting better and better.
I wake up with joy and love filling my heart.
Things are coming to me easily and effortlessly.
I am a radiant being filled with light and love.
My life is blossoming with true perfection.
Now, is the time, here is the place, and I am the one.
Starting now, I will live in loving, caring, sharing, trusting and spiritual ways.
I am applying my new joy filled, positive attitude this very day.

Some days, I would read the affirmations, but it was also effective listening to *my* words before I went to bed and my mind absorbed them subliminally, without my "itty bitty silly committee" judging them. You know the inner ones who say, You can't do *that* or you shouldn't feel *that* and you're afraid, and then you never try, but also by never trying, you never know.

I took a really cool typing job at an insurance company and I absolutely stunk at it. They wrote airplane policies for many famous people, through Lloyd's of London. I eventually realized that I would never be a fast, or even slightly accurate, typist and had to move on. But then I knew, that kind of job wasn't for me, and that was okay.

My daughter had a chance for a promotion at work, which added much more responsibilities and less free time. She wasn't sure if she would like that position.

I said, "Give it a try, if you don't like it, you can choose again!"

Sometimes I added the Lord's Prayer, just because I liked it and it was helpful.

> Our Father who art in Heaven
> Hallowed be the name,
> Thy kingdom come, thy will be done,
> on earth as it is in Heaven.
> Give us this day our daily bread
> and forgive us our trespasses,
> as we forgive those who trespass against us.
> Lead us not into temptation

but deliver us from evil.
For thine is the kingdom, the power
and the glory, forever and ever.
Amen.

I spoke on the tape with enthusiasm and joy in my voice and it was short enough to keep my attention and as I listened to it daily, changes and miracles appeared, effortlessly.
PS: I need a new car!

Chapter 4

My parents, Janet and Don, were married on Valentine's Day. This was my mom's favorite day.

It was even better than Christmas. It seemed the world stopped just for her to celebrate this glorious occasion. She planned the perfect anniversary surprise every year and kept my dad mesmerized.

She loved "love" and romance. She made her own wedding dress of delicate white satin. It had a modestly low, off-the-shoulder neckline, with a layer of puffy shoulder lace exposing the long sleeves. It fit her shape perfectly and gracefully flowed fully to the ground. She added a gently streaming three-foot train. She was stunning.

Her sisters, Jean and Joyce were the bridesmaids, with one dressed in a soft peach gown and the other in turquoise. They carried large bouquets of fabric flowers in the color of the other's dress. Her two brothers, Johnny and Jerry, were the groomsmen. They had a sweet flower girl and a handsome young ring bearer, and a best man. The men looked handsome in their black tuxedos, with black bow ties. Dad looked debonair and wore a white bow tie.

Dad was an only child, and he certainly acquired a large family after the nuptials. Her older brother James died in his youth from some kind of fever. She wanted to start a family of her own right away, and about a year and a half later, Mary came along.

Mom was a contestant on the *Queen For A Day*, television show.

The host inquired, "If you were queen for a day, what would you ask for?"

She answered, "I would like to have a new artificial leg for my husband."

Times were hard, and he was long overdue for a replacement. Years before, he lost his leg in a motorcycle accident. He hit some loose gravel and slid and the bike crushed his leg.

She was pregnant with her second child at that time, and of course, that would be me.

They asked her, "When are you expecting your baby?"

She giggled and said, "Any day now!"

She won the prize and my dad got a new leg. I used to go with him to the "wooden leg" store as I called it. I liked going on errands with my dad and he seemed to enjoy my company as I listened attentively to his stories. I don't remember Mary or Robbie ever going with us. They weren't much up for errands.

Once I dated a guy and that was his profession. He made artificial limbs and then would teach the patients how to continue on with their previous way of life. He taught them how to hike or ski or whatever they did, using the new limb. He created and shaped them to be the same as the other limb. I admired my friend's amazing talent and compassion.

My dad must have had the same type of instructor. "You may be slower at hiking, but you sure can do it!"

Mom and Dad also received a surprise gift of a night out on the town to a fancy restaurant and driven there in a fabulous limousine. She was so excited, but there was a problem.

She patted her stomach and said, "This is a wonderful gift, but as you can see, I can't use it right now, but I would love to able to go on my anniversary date, which is February 14."

The show's policy was that the prize had to be used right away, not three months later.

She got her wish and they even bought her a new dress for the occasion.

She shared with my dad afterward, "What a wonderful and romantic evening. I'll remember this night as long as I live."

There might as well have been no other dates on the calendar, because February 14, was "her" day, and she made it special for my dad too.

I felt like my dad and I were buddies.

When I was about five, I remembered he smoked all the time and I said, "Wow, Daddy, that is so neat, I want to smoke too."

He lifted me up on the kitchen counter. "Now, take a big drag." I couldn't believe he let me have a cigarette. I sucked it in, choked, turned green, nearly threw up, and never smoked again. He gave me that wise smile. I guess he always knew I would try it sometime, might as well get it over with.

Then there was the time I wanted to run away. He packed my suitcase for me and so I headed out. I would show him. We had a long, curving driveway, and I went down to the curb and sat there until dark then went back in.

Many years later, I was showing my daughter the large house I lived in with the long driveway. We arrived only to see something else. We looked at each other and started to laugh. The house was so small and the driveway barely could fit a compact car. I could envision my dad looking out the kitchen window, seeing me just sitting there on the curb, cooling my jets, and smiling.

It felt like my mom was my best friend. I liked her and trusted her. She had the most marvelous smile. I loved how she laughed and made everyone happy. She liked to curl my long blond hair, especially since I was such a tomboy. She gave the appearance of being only slightly angry when Mary cut my hair on Easter Sunday.

She surveyed the irreparable damage and said to me, "We have to fix this, and I saw this new pixie hairstyle in a magazine and it will look so cute on you."

I frowned when I saw the results, "I look like a boy."

She lovingly smiled. "Your hair will grow out and be just as pretty as before, no need to cry."

I was really upset by this short new "do" and wouldn't go inside the school when the bus dropped us off. My teacher gave me a scarf to wear and things were back to normal the next day and my hair *did* grow back. Boy, was my mom smart.

She made a beautiful slip for Mary and added pink hearts and wrote, "I love you" on the top of it. Mary was so happy, and she wore her special slip around the neighborhood as a summer dress.

I was always in bed real early when the tooth fairy was expected, who by coincidence, arrived on the first train in the evening. The railroad tracks were behind our house and I'm sure that regularly scheduled train could account for a lot of early bedtimes for the three of us. I was surprised when the tooth fairy always remembered to bring Mary and Robbie little treats also. So when I wanted to assist with the removal of Mary's teeth, that plan didn't go over too well.

Janet radiated love to everyone and helped anyone in trouble. Once, she found a wallet with six hundred dollars in it and took it to the police station.

My aunt Jean said, "Your mom would bring hobos in for dinner and collected every kind of scrap to help with the war recycling. She trusted everyone and was fearless. She always thought you were special and named you after her best friend, Patty."

I don't recall if I met or heard about her friend, but I felt special because of that choice. I learned early that best friends were to be loved and cherished and that would be true, forever.

One afternoon, we had a fire in our house, and she conscientiously scrambled to locate all of us in different parts of the house and tossed us out the door to safety. The chaos of the neighborhood and the fire trucks went unnoticed around us as she silently held my hand. We stood on the curb helplessly watching our house burn to the ground. Mary told me recently Mom had to go to the hospital for smoke inhalation. The electrical fire left nothing but a child's tricycle in the ashes. Then, thieves broke into the detached garage, in our absence, and stole everything else. Years later, I was telling my dad about this memory, just to verify the story.

He was greatly surprised, "I can't believe you remember those specific details, you were only about three years old.

I was six years old and at home with my mom. It was unusual for me to be home on a school day if I wasn't sick, and no one else was there. So I had my mom to myself and we could play dolls. She gave me the most wonderful doll for Christmas.

It didn't matter that the funny-looking man in the red suit kept saying, "Really, I'm not Uncle Johnny, I'm Santa and I'm bringing you this dolly."

I told him, "Only my mom knew I wanted this doll, and I didn't even tell Santa. I know this doll is from her."

Mary and Robbie were afraid of him and I told them, "It's only Uncle Johnny, why are you afraid?" (Although, he was a scary-looking Santa.) It seemed they were afraid of everything and would only try new things if I did it first. So when Mary got a twenty-six-inch bicycle for her birthday, she just stood there looking at it. A little too long in my opinion, so I jumped on the bike, even though I couldn't sit and reach the pedals and took it for a spin around the block. I soon found out why curbs were useful—they stopped the bike!

My mom answered the phone and I sat down beside her as she talked to her friend. I played quietly with my doll. A moment later, she slowly fell to the floor. I didn't know what happened and I shook her and tried to wake her up.

I cried, "Mom, wake up," but she didn't move.

I picked up the phone and told the lady, "My mom fell off the chair and is asleep and won't wake up."

I never saw her again. No one told me she had died and was never coming back.

I asked my dad, "What happened? I was being quiet." I begged him, "Make her come back. I'll be good, I promise, I won't tease Robbie anymore, tell her I'm sorry, make her come back."

The following year was a blank. Aunt Jean, one of my favorites, told me, "You sat on the end of the bed and cried, and waited every day, for her to come home."

No one told me what happened, and I had no idea why my dad kept taking us to the cemetery. The truth is always easier, no matter how hard it is to accept, than not knowing. Her illness made her heart give out.

I wondered many times over the years how I happened to be home alone with her that day. I asked my dad later and he said, "It *was* odd, I have tried to think back and I don't know why you weren't in school or where your sister and brother were at that time. I can't remember, but it is curious."

Apparently, my mom had been sick and in and out of hospitals for many years. I never remembered that.

When Mom's life was nearing the end, she refused to make her transition until she had one last anniversary celebration with her husband. She hung on for months and died, February 15, and then, decades later, after the harmful effects of smoking, when it was Dad's time, he waited also, and died on February 16. Even in death, he wouldn't spoil "her" day. He loved her that much.

Just pondering, Dad was born in twenty, Mom was married at twenty. Dad married at twenty-eight and Mom died at twenty-eight. He was eight years older and they were married eight years. Hmmm?

I never realized my mom was that sick. I only remembered her joyful disposition, which evidently changed and took its toll as she got sicker. She was a loving, happy influence on me. My concerns as a youngster were far more pressing—like how could I sneak behind the couch to watch TV while quarantined with measles?

Apparently, my mom felt she was going to die young and the doctor told her that having children could possibly shorten her life considerably, but it would complete her life as well. There was no way she would follow those intolerable instructions. Maybe that's why Mary, Robbie and I are so close in age.

As I look back, even as young as I was, I realized she was preparing me for many future experiences. Years later, as I progressed on my spiritual path and witnessed, with pure certainty, what I would call miracles, my mom "visited" me.

She reminded me of our spiritual prearranged agreement, "I asked *you*, to be there with me, that day." It's still as vivid now as it was then.

Chapter 5

I WASN'T ALWAYS SO LUCKY in love. I never found "Mr. Right" to go along with "Ms. Left" (me), the yin to my yang, the one partner who was going in the same direction and had the same enthusiasm for life as I had. I wanted a boyfriend to go to church with and work on humanitarian projects together. I wished for an equal, caring, sharing, loving, compassionate, and spiritual partner. He must be out there somewhere. I kept wishing.

When I met Mark, I thought he was the "one." He felt so familiar. The first time I saw him, I was crushing on him right away. I thought he was so cool. It was his first day with the company I worked for. He drove up in a shiny black Camero, and I watched as he backed into a parking space near the front of the building. He was wearing nice, brown slacks and a striped, long-sleeved shirt with a complimenting tie under his corduroy jacket vest. I watch him intently as he leisurely strolled into the office. He was tall and had the longest legs and a cute, Magnum PI, backside!

The company's eighteen bank branches were being centralized to one main office in Southern California and the other eighteen were going to San Francisco.

It was my job to go from branch to branch and help organize them for the move. The individual branches stayed open until ready to move, one by one. I didn't see Mark during that time but patiently waited for his branch to be relocated to the new facility.

When he finally arrived, we became close friends immediately. We were always together, and though we were opposites in every way, we got along very well. He was tall and I was short. I was positive and outgoing while he was quiet and shy. We worked together for many years and rotated positions as supervisor of the department. We played softball on our company's team, he was the pitcher and I was the catcher. I was manager of our team one year and he was the next.

I remember the time when I was the next batter up and had the bat leaning over my shoulder as I approached the bag. Apparently I was in a daze as I waited for my turn. The ball was headed for home plate at a fast pace, and I quickly raised my hand for cover, so the speeding ball wouldn't hit me in the face. But it landed in my gloveless hand. Oh my gosh, I immediately dropped the ball, but it was too late. Everyone on the team noticed, not the amazing catch I just made, but that our ball was still in play and our runner was out.

"Why did you do *that*?" they hollered.

"Are you kidding? I couldn't catch another ball like that if I was wearing a glove the size of Texas."

There was no romantic involvement between us for a few years, but we remained timeless best friends.

My co-workers prompted, "Why don't you both get married, you belong together."

His mom said, "You two are so connected, you must have been together in a past life."

I loved him deeply over the years.

One summer, Mark and his brother and a few friends rented a vacation house in Newport Beach for the week. It was right on the boardwalk, and I went down there for a few days. It was the coolest place I've ever stayed. We joined in the volleyball game and played until dark, drank wine in the moonlight, had a somewhat romantic evening on the secluded beach, and talked for hours. What a fabulous evening. I enjoyed his company, and I daydreamed about our relationship going to the next level.

I loved the idea of beach living. This week had spoiled me.

I told Mark, "I want a place just like this, on the water, somewhere really neat."

He laughed at me and made fun of my frivolous words. I guess since he knew the expense of the week, maybe this was just a pie in the sky idea? I think not!

I was offended by his attitude and pronounced, "Have you ever heard me make a statement like that, without making it happen?"

He stopped in his tracks and agreed, "No, I haven't."

It bothered him that I was so ambitious. He liked the simple life. He was Mr. "Short Tax Form," while I had rental properties and children and other things, and I was Ms. "Long Tax Form!"

So I started my beach house quest. I checked out property around that area and had to go to "Plan B" fast when I realized I couldn't even afford the down payment. I selected a more practical location.

I used to take my children on vacation to visit relatives in Texas, and on the ride home, I drove as far as I could in one day, so the last day's drive would be easier and we always wound up in Lake Havasu City, Arizona. We unpacked our tents and sleeping bags and stayed on the shore of the lake in the campground.

I wrote myself a "house at the river" note, like that book by Og Mandino suggested. I think it was, *The Greatest Miracle in the World*, but I read several of his books. I declared my intention very clearly.

"By this date, my income will be such and such and I will have my place at the river." I signed and dated the note and put it away.

This project would probably take a few years. I needed to keep a clear focus but also not be attached to the outcome, so it could manifest in any way that was for my highest good, but also, so I wouldn't limit any serendipitous opportunity that presented itself. I would "move my feet" and follow the logical path that would lead me to my new home.

Mark and I went to Florida on vacation. We had a place close to Disney World and had a busy day of walking, standing in long lines to ride as many rides as possible, and sampling several beers from the different countries. So after this splendid day, we went back to the condo and I decided to take a wonderful, soothing bath in the oversized Jacuzzi tub before dinner. He was in the other room and I got the bath ready.

I dropped in the tiniest amount of fragrant bubbles, and in a blink, there were zillions of bubbles exploding everywhere and continuing to mount.

He came in and was astounded, "What happened?"

I couldn't stop laughing. He grabbed the trash bucket and started scooping and bailing. I was rolling in the floor while trying to capture this bubble monster on film. He filled up the shower with buckets full of froth from the tub. His face was bright red as he worked feverishly to control this expanding bubble machine. It was equally comical watching this normally slow-paced guy start whirling around like a dervish and not knowing what to do next to stop this fiasco.

We had spent lots of fun times together over the years, and I hoped we would marry someday. He had been married previously and didn't have any children, or want them, but he was always good to my kids. He was such a decent guy.

Jeni was on the high school soccer team, and they had an awards program one evening. She was an excellent player and her team was getting a trophy. I enjoyed watching the games as well as running up and down the field cheering them on. They were tied and went into kickoffs. Player after player matched each shot. It was Jeni's turn to be the tie-breaker. She carefully went to the ball and sized up the goalie. Her face showed a clear strategy. I was snapping pictures of this suspenseful moment as it unfolded in slow motion. She backed up and ran to the ball and gave it a deliberate kick. It hit the top corner of the goal post and fell into the net and they won the game. She had done that trick before at the very last second or being the last player and made the goal almost every time.

Both of my children started playing soccer when they were five, and I liked the idea that everyone got to play, unlike some other sports. I went to all their games, as well as practices. My son Alan played soccer also, but his love was baseball. Their separate schedules were convenient most of the time because of the seven-year difference in their ages. They usually got to play on close together fields, in the same city, or their game times were back to back. So for many years of being the chauffer, banner maker, team mom, or snack person, I didn't have to juggle games often.

Jeni's first team when she was a little tot was called the Froggers. The kids would huddle around the ball and all you could see was tiny feet kicking and kicking, and the ball never moved. But finally, when the pack of little bodies moved, the ball moved as well and eventually made its way to the other end of the field and sometimes even went into the net.

Alan's team called the Red Devils, on the other hand, were serious about the game and winning, and equally as exciting to watch.

Her awards ceremony came to an end and the team wore big smiles, as bright as their trophies. We walked out of the auditorium together. I was talking to Jeni, and when she turned her head to listen to her friend, I immediately fell down the high school steps, right in front of everyone.

Jeni ran down the stairs and was mortified. She couldn't believe I fell down the stairs in front of her teammates. Oh yeah, like I really enjoyed myself?

She tried to pick me up and kept saying, "Mom, get up!"

I hesitantly replied, "I can't get up, I think I broke my leg."

The next day at school, her friends asked her, "Wasn't that your mom who fell down the steps?"

Surprisingly, we did survive that embarrassing catastrophe.

Mark decided to move to Arizona and give up the wild rat race and live the simple life on the lake.

His brother Jess had some time off work and visited him in Arizona. I joined them since I would be laid up for a while. I was hobbling around on crutches with a badly sprained leg. Fortunately it wasn't broken. I couldn't do much and appreciated them nurturing me back to health.

Jess was a professional chef, and I was glad for this chance to be off work and be pampered by these two hunks. His meals were to die for.

It was Valentine's Day and Jess and I were on the balcony, watching the sunset and waiting for Mark, who was running late from work. It was the first time he bought me a present on this date and acknowledged loving me, in front of his brother.

We had been in an intimate relationship for years now, and I knew he loved me, but he didn't express it out loud until then. I was pleasantly surprised.

Jess, in his spare time, was a minister and did weddings and he always wanted to marry us. I kept waiting.

After a short while, I went back to work but couldn't make it up the stairs to the accounting department on my crutches. I suggested I take more time off, but they wanted me to come back to work which was good because I needed the money. So I had the temporary title of receptionist.

This was a large company and they had important visitors every day. I liked greeting the guests and directing them to the meeting area. When they had out-of-town meetings, I had limited social opportunities, since everyone was gone or worked upstairs. I was bored beyond belief. There was a greeting board that announced who our special guest or company would be and it changed daily. I decided to create a unique message to greet the guests. I had plenty of time to lay out the letters across my desk and spell out anything I felt inspired to say that day. I would be wildly creative every day and my sayings became the anticipated talk of the day. The president of the company started coming down every morning to read the new words on the board… "Your smile is like peanut butter, you have to spread it around." He looked over at me with that grin of approval and was proud as his guests were welcomed in such an unusual way.

He said, "It's too bad your leg is getting better and you'll be leaving this desk! Everyone will miss your greetings!"

I worked there until that big earthquake hit and I found that multi-storied, glass buildings didn't work for me. I was literally shaking in my boots. Buildings were crumbling and my mobile home…was.

I called my dad, who recently moved not too far away and asked, "Can I spend the night at your house?"

He replied, "Certainly." He spent the evening calling everyone to announce, "Guess who's afraid of earthquakes and staying here tonight?"

No one guessed it was me.

I shrugged my shoulders and said, "Hey, it's not my *fault*!"

It was time for me to move to Arizona. Mark and I moved in together. We were still such good friends and shared chores and expenses. Whoever was home first started dinner and the other did the dishes. There was never a discussion of "It's not my job," or "the game's on," as I heard in other relationships. He was a considerate person.

My dad and stepmom came to visit and she said, "Did you ever notice that he never swears in front of women?" I gave that some thought because I had heard him with the guys. He was a man's man but still respected women and I appreciated that. I still had the idea of marriage in my head.

We were going on ten years and I mentioned marriage to him. He declared, "I don't want to get married, things will change."

I was shocked by his attitude.

"WHAT?" I huffed back. "What can possibly change? We have lived together for years. You have seen me on my best and absolute worst days and we play together so well."

He said, "I was married before and it didn't work out and my parents were divorced, and you were divorced."

He was basing our whole relationship on things in the past and wasn't even considering "us," as a future, just a permanent live-in friend?

He said, "It doesn't matter if we are married or not."

"Well, it matters to me, if you don't care enough for me after all this time to commit to me and be my husband, then I need to move on."

But what made that decision easier for me was when I was buying a washer and dryer and asked him if he wanted to pay for half, he said, "What if we break up, who will get them?"

"Good grief, we are *not* talking about children!"

He would rather pay me to use the washer and dryer than to commit to our future. Every load he did, he put coins there, and every time he did, I got more resentful.

"You are just being stupid and selfish."

After a while, he moved out and I started dating, and he asked me, "Are you going to marry that guy?"

"I'm not shopping for a husband, I don't *need* to be married, I wanted to be married, to *you*."

He sent me a card recently with two cute puppies playing and the caption was, "Friends are presents you give yourself." We did remain friends, and after thirty years, we still occasionally go on road trips together. He was always my fun play buddy!

Chapter 6

How would I make my place on the water dream come true? I was cognizant of the results I wanted and had the universe work on it with me. First of all, I needed to make more money to be able to afford this house, even if it meant taking a class for new training. I put my name in the hat for another position that paid more. I filled a jar of dirt and kept it on my desk. This represented the land I would be buying. I found a nice floor plan of a model home and took it home and kept it visible.

Sure enough, little by little, pieces of this plan began to effortlessly appear.

I got funny reactions about this whole process.

Several people thought I was nuts in the beginning and asked, "Why have you got a jar of dirt on your desk?"

"Oh, that's my beach house."

They teased me, "Is a house going to grow in the dirt like in Jack and the Beanstalk?"

Shortly afterward, I found a wonderful piece of land sitting high up the side of a hill in Lake Havasu. My great view was the London Bridge and the activity-filled lake. In the background was the old airport. I always had a vision of flying a plane over that airport, circling up to the runway, but not landing. But a new airport was built on the east side of town, so I couldn't wait to see how that unfolded.

There was a huge rock on the property near the street that was calling me. I asked the realtor about the price. He was surprised that I inquired about that property.

He said, "The price has just been lowered because no one likes that rock."

I thought it had character and was perfect for the driveway to wrap around, making the drive to the house less steep.

I designed the house I wanted and had the plans professionally drawn up.

I informed the builder, "This house has to be done by this specific date."

He acknowledged my guidelines, "No problem, that's plenty of time."

I drove out on weekends to check on the progress, and for months, he hadn't even broke ground yet, but kept saying, "No problem."

Well, there was a problem, and I wasn't reassured one bit as my personal deadline approached.

I stated, "Your schedule in not acceptable, there is no way my house will be done in a satisfactory manner in the amount of time you have left."

I didn't understand why he didn't take me seriously. He gave me a refund for the money I paid to him, all except for the plans and he kept them. (He did build that house, in town, using my plans and it looked great! Maybe it was just the steep hill that was a problem?)

I liked that street that overlooked the lake and was disappointed with the builder. I wanted that to be my retirement home and hopefully it would be paid off by then. It had to be uniquely special and that's why I chose to build and not buy because the model homes all looked the same.

I still had my "house at the river" dream, and once again, I had to go to "Plan B."

Jeni inquired when Plan A fell apart, "What is Plan B?"

"I don't know yet, but I'm sure it will come to me."

I never had an actual Plan B worked out beforehand because then Plan A would be so rigid and it made it a plan to fail. If it didn't work, the idea of knowing that Plan B was on the back burner, just in case, gave me the initiative to create another idea that would work. It let me be flexible and go with the flow. But I always had the foundation for the idea clearly established and I knew the final outcome. So when unexpected changes occurred, I changed also.

A few months back, I bought a boat and hauled it back and forth to enjoy the Arizona lake on weekends, while I hunted for my new house. I took a leisurely spin on the lake and returned to the dock after a few hours. I loaded my boat onto the trailer that was gracefully floating at the edge of the water. All of a sudden, the rubber bow stopper that kept the boat from driving into my back seat fell off the trailer and into the water, but the boat kept going forward.

The boat caught on the now bare metal frame and gouged out an unattractive design about two feet long on each side of the bow. I was stunned and upset. How could *that* happen? I loaded and unloaded that boat a hundred times by myself.

I planned to tow the boat back to California like I did every weekend and I was so disgusted I decided to leave it there to get it fixed and pick it up on the next trip. It wasn't a real expensive repair, but I sure carried on like it was.

I drove around the area to "cool off" before I got on the road for the five-hour drive home. I noticed a sign advertising brand-new condos for sale across the street from the lake. I had no intention of buying a condominium, but since it would waste some time and possibly give me some fresh ideas, I took a peek. It was a brand-new complex and the lake and marina were close by. The swaying palm trees created the atmosphere of Hawaii. I looked around and thought maybe *this* was Plan B? There were only a few units that had sold and I had the pick of several. I checked out each unit on the top floor that faced the lake. I sat in each condo and visually measured and thought some more. I like a lot of space and these were large two bedroom condos, which was perfect for weekend getaways. I could have a pool and spa and fabulous landscaping and a maintenance crew to keep it up while I was away. This idea seemed quite acceptable, practical, and cost-effective.

I told the on-sight salesperson, "I need to think this over. Please hold all of these units for me (without a deposit) and I'll decide by Thursday which one I want."

He looked at me with that funny look I'd seen before, the one that conveyed, "Surely she's kidding!" I was serious. It had to "feel" right, and I would be back. I did a lot of thinking and as I drove home.

The sales agent and I became friends and we laughed about that later, when he recalled, "I'm holding several condos, without a deposit, and she'll be back!"

I drove home with a satisfied mind that I made the right decision. I would go back and physically measure each unit, since the layouts varied slightly.

I needed to see what location got the most sun. It would be extremely hot in the summer and I wondered how much light I would lose to protect me from the heat.

I was amongst the weekender vehicles that were going home from Las Vegas or the river and about an hour and a half from my home. I was climbing over a hill, when I heard screeching and crashing ahead. Something was happening and it sounded ghastly. Cars were slamming into each other and the big trucks began to jackknife. In that moment, everything ran through my head. In my driver's training class as a teen, I was taught to always leave a "way out" on the road. Since I wasn't towing my boat, I could honk to get attention and veer off to the left side of the road easily to create a break in the traffic. The cars behind had those extra seconds to react to my horn and miss the accident, and that was exactly what happened.

I sat there and caught my breath and realized if I had been pulling my boat, most likely, I would have died or caused critical injuries because my boat would have been airborne in that type of situation and the people all around me would have been in serious danger.

Thank you, guardian angels.

I went back to the condo complex that next week and sat in each room of every unit that met my guidelines. But none of them felt right and I couldn't place the feeling, but knew I hadn't found the right one yet.

I spotted a small sign that advertised a three-bedroom for sale. There was only one three bedroom in the whole complex and it was the developer's. He added several amenities and it was nice. He had a stroke and couldn't get up the stairs and had to sell it. He never lived in it and I asked to see it.

The salesman, who had saved the two-bedroom units until I returned, was trying to dissuade me, then. It was a quiet, adult complex and I was a relatively young, single woman, who would be there generally on weekends. (You know how those people from LA are!) He expected I would have wild parties and disrupt the other residents. He felt more secure if I purchased a two-bedroom, as it seemed less likely I could have too many visitors at once. But this one was perfect. I liked a quiet place and privacy.

I walked in and looked around and said, "This is the one, wrap it up."

He sure was surprised when the escrow closed in a few days.

The condo was located in the corner and appeared deceivingly small from the front door. But it wrapped around and had three separate entrances to the extra rooms that could be locked off and separated, as desired. The view was magnificent and it wasn't in direct sunlight for long periods. I had a detached garage and a covered parking space next to it, which were close to the main entrance.

I met a handicapped couple who owned the only parking space big enough to accommodate my boat. It was way in the back and quite a distance from their house.

I asked, "Would you like to trade parking spaces, you can have mine by your house and I could have yours, out in the boonies."

The elderly man waved his cane gently in the air.

"Yes, I would love that! How much money are you asking for the trade?"

"No money, just convenience."

I never locked the boat trailer when I headed back to California and it worried my neighbor, Ed.

It was so refreshing not to have to lock up and tie everything down, like in California. He watched over it like a mother hen.

One day, he came over with a picture of my boat. "This is what your boat looked like."

I replied, "What? I don't get it."

He smiled and said, "Just in case it gets stolen, you can describe it to the police!" He cracked me up. So I bought a trailer hitch lock. One of the other neighbors made a set of chocks for my tires. I liked my new friends.

Mark threw a big birthday party for me and I got all the usual over-the-hill gag gifts. He put an ad in the newspaper, with one of my childhood pictures, "Patty cake, Patty cake, forty years old, now you can be sure that everyone's been told!" It was the older folks being the wild ones and I laughed until my face hurt. Well at least now, I got the gag gift of ageless face cream to cover up these new lines.

My next-door neighbors, Mel and Audry, put black balloons all over my exterior door for my birthday. One time I borrowed an egg from her and couldn't return it for a week.

When I did, Mel said, "There is nothing that made Audry happier, than someone who returns borrowed things and boy, does she love you."

I decided to live in my Arizona condo year round. It was better than fighting a two-hour commute, to only go thirty miles to work in California, I found a job as a property manager and it was a great job. After a while, I earned a cool raise, which was not money, but a large picture window in my office, across the street from the lake!

Years ago, I had a sales job and I went to Lake Havasu to make sales and then play. I had a jade stone that I carried in my pocket, for luck and prosperity. I was doing my routine sales calls and my inspirational stone fell out of my pocket and was lost. I loved that rock and searched everywhere. It was also a worry stone—rub it and don't worry. I never found it but laughed at the thought, what better place to lose my prosperity stone!

But there I was once again, standing on the exact spot where I lost that stone, managing the property for the millionaire who owned it. What are the odds?

I had another sales job and took prospective clients on tours of the area. I made the most interesting sales. I had a silly sales pitch, more to entertain myself, I think.

One lady, who was not impressed and cranky due to the heat, said, "I hear it gets up to 120 degrees here."

I replied, "Absolutely not."

She had a sigh of relief that the rumor wasn't true. I continued, "It gets as high as 128."

She burst into laughter and I think that was the first time her husband heard her laugh out loud like that!

One sale was so strange, I'll never forget it.

I had the perspective buyers in my office, signing the final papers. The normally sparkling clean lake had some sort of bacteria spill from a houseboat and helicopters were flying over, using their infrared equipment, to monitor the situation. As they sat at my desk, the air conditioner broke overhead and water started flooding down from the ceiling and into the trash can that I quickly grabbed.

My boss pulled me aside and said, "You need to keep them here for a while longer."

"Why? They have been here all day already."

He said, "There is a bomb scare in their hotel and they can't go back there yet."

I just looked at my clients and put my hands in the air and shook my head in disbelief. I was ready to tear up their contract and send them on their way.

They came back the next day, and everyone knew they would be back to cancel the sale and not one salesperson would have disagreed with them.

They were leaving town and wanted to stop by and say, "Thank you for the great tour and we are quite satisfied with this deal because nothing else could possibly happen here."

I took several people out in a golf cart to show them around the resort. We drove around the magnificent London Bridge, a wonder in itself, and I told the story of this incredible feat. The folks were captivated by my knowledge.

I informed them, "After this bridge was delivered and painstakingly put back into working order, stone by stone, the owner realized they delivered the wrong bridge." The tourists gasped in amazement.

I continued, "But he couldn't send it back because he threw out the receipt." I love sales tours!

Many years later, I was moving and as I unpacked several boxes, a sheet of paper fell out of a book. I read the note and a huge smile broke out on my face. It was the "house at the river" note that I listed my intentions, dated and signed my promise, and put it away for the universe to work out the details. Everything, I had written down had manifested within *two* weeks of the date I chose back then, *and* in a way I would have never imagined.

Chapter 7

A LADY NAMED LORENE CAME to live with us as a live-in housekeeper. I didn't care much for her. She seemed to me like a troublemaker, and everything she did seemed questionable. I saw my relatives less and less, and I wondered why.

Shortly afterward, she told Don that Robbie and I were having serious emotional problems. He was twisting his hair and I was sucking my fingers, and crying all the time.

Don told my aunt Jean, "I took the kids to the school psychologist. He recommended an immediate change of environment for them."

"What does that mean?" Jean asked.

He continued, "He said since Mary was older, she understood the situation better and was doing okay."

Don and Lorene were married when I was about seven. Mary called her mom right away. I never did, nor would I ever. She was not *my* mom.

Jean wrote to Mary in later years, "I thought that Don hoped his new marriage would provide the recommended change of environment to help the kids with their emotional problems. But from then on, every time we visited, Patty and Robbie were supposedly away visiting friends or relatives."

Mary had been reading all of these old letters and now passing the information on to me.

Mary read on, "After a while it was getting puzzling to all of us. Grandma Regina (Janet and Jean's mom) was the first to sense the strangeness of it all."

Grandma Regina always tried to see us on birthdays and holidays.

"Gradually, the rest of us began to sense it too, and when we tried to question Don, it was obvious he didn't want to talk and soon we believed they just didn't want us around too often and didn't give much further thought about how strange it was."

No one knew what was going on.

Jean continued, "Then one day, Don wrote me a letter asking me to notify Grandma Regina and the rest of the family that he had placed Patty and Robbie up for adoption earlier and it was final now. Believe me all of us were absolutely stunned. We never had any other explanation from Don and could never understand why he couldn't have discussed the adoption with us before he did it."

The whole family was heartbroken.

Jean added, "He must have known we would have taken Patty and Robbie to live with us for as long as he felt it best. We gladly took care of all three of you for five or six weeks one time in an emergency. Even with my four kids, one being a new baby, we were able to manage. Besides that, Grandma Regina would have eagerly taken them to live with her. He had to know how much she loved them. Johnny (Jean's brother) and Adele desperately wanted children and were already considering the possibility of adopting. They were absolutely sick when they learned the news. They loved all of you so much."

Nothing seemed justifiable.

I quizzed Mary, "Did you know we were adopted out when relatives came to visit?"

"Yes," she responded.

"What did you tell them, when they asked where we were?"

"I have no idea of what I may have told them."

I felt deceived, knowing she knew all along and she kept it a secret from our grandmas and relatives.

"What did Dad and Lorene tell you about the adoption?" I asked.

"That Robbie went to a co-worker's home and you went to Leota and Hymie's." Simple as that, here today and gone tomorrow.

I asked her, "Did you wonder if you might be next?"

"Not that I remember."

This was so weird. It was as if one day, out of the blue, he put up an ad on his bulletin board at work. "Free, one little kid, come get her quick!" I was adopted out so fast, they packed my sister's clothes by mistake, and when I unpacked at this strange new place, I didn't even have my clothes or anything that fit me. In addition, I had a broken arm from falling off the monkey bars, trying to skip two bars backward!

This is how the adoptees came into play. Obviously the bulletin board worked for Robbie. He was adopted by a co-worker after I was gone. Lorene's daughter, Martha, had a schoolmate, Sarah, whose parents were best friends with Leota and Hymie, my new parents. Then wait, there's more. Lorene's grandson, Frank, was adopted into their family and became Mary's new brother.

My grandma Geraldine (my dad's mom) was mortified and devastated. She told me, "Don't tell the neighbors about this." As if I could even explain it. I never told any of my schoolmates. So my new life was now private.

Why was I sent away and why did it have to be a secret? Why did they keep Mary? Maybe she wouldn't cause any problems, like I might have.

I asked Mary once, "Did you ever fight with Lorene?"

She said, "I talked back to her once when I was in high school."

"What happened?" I inquired.

"She slapped me."

"What did you do then?"

She answered, "I never did it again."

Mary was raised to be perfect, there was no second best. Boy, what pressure. I heard stories of how Lorene berated Mary and I felt bad for her. One time, Lorene asked Mary for money for her dad's oxygen. Mary had a family of twelve and barely making ends meet but sent them $10.

Lorene was offended and sent it back to her and said, "Keep it, that amount won't help us." I couldn't believe my ears. Lorene's daughter was well off; why didn't she ask her?

Mary told me about a memory she has carried with her. She was two months pregnant with her last child and maybe weighed 113 pounds. Lorene told her *twice* how disgusting she was. Then Dad wrote in her autograph book, the one from Disneyland, "Here's to my daughter, who eats more than she otter, but in spite of her habits, she's cuter than rabbits and tries to be good like we taught her."

Mary sadly said, "It was a puzzle to me."

I was eight when the adoption was being finalized. I was petrified as I sat in the judge's chambers on that cold, brown, leather couch.

He asked me, "How do you feel about this adoption?"

Inside I was saying, "What do you mean, how do I feel? I want to go home. I want *my* family, not these strangers." I was immobilized, my words and emotions were tucked away, since I didn't have a choice anyway, I was barely able to breathe, let alone, feel.

I hesitantly answered, "Okay, I guess."

On the drive home, my new dad stopped abruptly at a yellow light and I fell to the floor in the back seat. I actually slid gently but that incident gave me the chance to cry, and cry, I did.

Hymie was a nice guy and showered me with anything he thought I needed and tried to make my new life happy. Leota, my new mom, was mean. She would grab a switch off the fig tree and give it to me good for the serious offense of biting my nails or spilling the trash. I didn't ever recall being in such trouble that required a switch to correct my behavior. I never heard of a switch. I'm sure my real parents spanked me for being mischievous, but nothing like this.

She said over and over again, "I didn't want you. You are only here because Hymie wanted children."

If she caught me sucking my fingers at night, she made me sit out in the front yard in a straight chair, sucking my fingers, so everyone could see my disgusting habit. She wanted be to be humiliated.

Why didn't *anyone* help to protect me when I was being beaten? I realized then, it was up to me, to take care of myself. I can't even count how many times I was "saved" by divine intervention. I may have called it angels, faith, intuition, ESP, or whatever, but I know, without a doubt, it was God protecting and looking after *me*.

Thank you, God.

When I was ten, I had just about enough of Leota and I ran away. I couldn't figure out why she was so mean, or why my real family didn't want me anymore. Maybe I was trouble? I filled my lunch pail with a change of clothes and took a few dollars that Leota had stashed away and started off on my bicycle. I had no idea or sense of direction where I would go, but I knew I needed to go somewhere safe.

I had ridden my bike for hours and was getting very tired and got off and started walking my bike. I passed an old man out watering his lawn.

My impression of the look on his face was "Why is that girl walking that nice bike? My granddaughter would like to have a bike like that and would be riding it."

Obviously, he was concerned I was out alone and far from any neighborhood. But I left my bike in front of his fence for his granddaughter and kept walking. (Leota was furious about that.)

I walked for hours and looked around for a place to rest, and to my great surprise, I recognized Grandma Geraldine's street. I couldn't believe my eyes. How did I get here? I hadn't seen my grandma in two years. I rushed down the block to her house and rang the doorbell. She opened the door and started to cry and grabbed me up in her arms.

She looked around for a car. "Where are your parents?"

I said, "They aren't here, I ran away."

She assumed I was teasing until I lifted my shirt and showed her the evidence of that darn fig tree branch. She was horrified and called my real dad and the police came and I was taken to juvenile hall for a few days. I didn't like being locked up one bit. It wasn't like prison, and I was treated well, but locked up tight at night wasn't for me. I stayed at Aunt Jean's for a few months, until Leota calmed down. Then it was back to the same old way of life. I ran away a few more times.

Leota advised me, "If you run away one more time, you will be sent to juvenile hall, and locked up forever." I decided I better just stay put. I would be eighteen in a few years and then I could move on.

Hymie owned a gas station located at a very busy intersection. The turning cars would speed around the corner. I often thought about running in front of one of those cars, so I could end this miserable life. I didn't know how I could possibly wait until I was old enough to move out.

But then, I always had another immediate thought, "That wouldn't be fair to the person who accidentally hit me, and by my actions, I would be ruining their life and that wasn't right."

I don't know where that logic came from, but it sure saved me.

It was quite an ordeal, but the most amazing thing to me is, to this *very* day, as a well-traveled adult, I still have no sense of direction and can't find my grandma's house, without a map, or today, without a GPS!

Thank you, guardian angels!

I think my only fight with my dad started because he was trying to find redemption before he died. It was my stepmom's eightieth birthday and my stepsister called to invite me to her party.

Then she added, "Since you are coming, can you help with some of the expenses? All of mom's family will be there." I could afford it and agreed to help.

As soon as I hung up, I began fuming. Why was I even going, or agreeing to pay, for anything? I wasn't close to her, and I always blamed her. I was still upset she had moved into my house, and then moved me out so quickly. I was angry because I didn't get to see my grandparents or Mary and Robbie for ten years.

I never got to discuss the adoption with my dad and I thought it had to be her who ignited the firestorm. I defended my dad if anyone badmouthed him. I didn't want to believe he could do what he did, without any explanation, or guilt being required.

My dad's health was declining, and he started writing me letters. They started, "Dear Janet." He was writing love letters to me, as if I was his previous wife. The letters had no return address and were sealed and taped shut with postage tape. I was confused.

"Remember that romantic date we had and how your brother Jerry barged in?"

He started getting more intimate and the letters made me very uncomfortable. I asked him to stop. I thought he must be regressing or getting dementia since he was so sick and I let it pass. Then, he started writing to me about his relationship with Lorene with specific details, knowing that I would never stand for that.

But what really set me off was when he said, "Don't tell anyone about my letters."

The timing was perfect. I called him up and confronted him about the letters and the party.

I was enraged, "I won't be going to her party, with *her* family. I don't know most of those people and they aren't my family. My family was stolen from me, and *you* were the robber. I will never forget what *you* did."

I kept venting, "You and Lorene came around after high school and acted like everything was fine, and I wanted you back. I wanted my dad back in my life. But where were you when I was growing up and needed help? Where were you when I graduated? I had *no* one there on my big day. Where were you when I was moments away from being attacked, by a relative you forced on me? Where were you when I was getting married and asked you to walk me down the aisle because Hymie had moved away and wasn't going to be there? You answered, 'I won't be there, your grandma is sick.'

"You're not coming to *my* wedding?"

"I had to have my best friend from high school walk me down the aisle, and then, you showed up acting like nothing was wrong."

"But your grandma was sick and I didn't think I could make it, but she got better."

"Well, to me, there was no acceptable excuse."

I kept on, "Where were you when your adult son, Robbie, wanted to reunite with you and you sent him away?" You said, "He's not my responsibility, especially if he has emotional problems. Why were you so mean to Mary when she was an adult and had a large family? She wasn't asking you to financially support her."

He fell silent, and I knew our relationship was over. I had hoped over the years that this issue would be reconciled before he died.

Maybe he would explain or apologize, but that was never the case. And what happened then, he died.

Mary told me one day, "Dad always liked you more, even after the adoption. He never disagreed with anything you did and was proud of you."

"How can you even say that? You had the best life."

Lorene wanted Mary to land the perfect husband and be the best wife and mother, and she unfortunately was groomed for years but chose a different direction, for herself.

Then, it dawned on me, her being left behind was just as harmful and nerve-racking as us being sent away. She must have been on pins and needles all the time, having to be perfect, waiting for her turn to get the boot, or not. All three of us were affected in such different and dramatic ways.

Chapter 8

NOW FOR SOME AWED (ODDS) and ends. I lived in a house that had a pool and decided to have a party. I was preparing for the event and placed every towel from the linen closet by the sliding glass door that led out to the pool.

My friend Rene asked, "What are you doing? Everyone will bring their own towels."

I answered, "I don't know why, but I feel like we will need them."

I continued getting ready for guests.

I often got flashes of intuition that didn't make sense then, but I did listen, just in case.

Well, one of the guys was carrying a glass beer bottle and while horsing around, he slipped and landed on the broken glass. He severely cut an artery in his arm and blood was spurting everywhere. I quickly grabbed towel after towel and packed and bandaged his arm and we headed for the hospital.

The doctor said, "Good thinking to use those towels, you probably saved his life."

The ordeal took hours, and we were covered in blood by day's end. He was stitched up and would be fine, and all ended well. Thanks to the towel "heads up"!

*****

I had a Siamese cat named Molly and she followed me everywhere. I dressed her up in doll clothes and bonnets and paraded her around in my doll carriage. I could tell by the cat's squirming she hated it, but she indulged me and let me take her for a brief stroll.

When she had kittens, she brought all six of them into my bed every night and laid them by my side.

She did this with each litter. It annoyed Leota, who put them back in the box under the bed and made sure they couldn't get out. Molly waited and watched for her to go back to bed and one by one, she grabbed each tiny kitten in her mouth and jumped up on my bed and put it under my covers. She brought me the whole Kit and Kaboodle! Molly "saved" me during many rough times and I believed we had a unique connection, even if she was just a cat.

*****

I wanted to be on TV when I was young and saw an ad that stated auditions were being held for child roles in commercials. I didn't have any talent, or parental permission, but decided to call anyway. You know, like writing your own absent note, "Please excuse Sally from school today. Love, Mom."

I was on TV when I was little, but my mom made me get off because I was scratching the set!

Did you see me in the movies, I go quite often!

*****

My young nephew heard that story and jumped in, "If you were on TV, you could be rich!" he exclaimed.

He was constantly looking for any edge that made him rich, by hook or by crook.

I advised him, "You can be rich without having a lot of money."

He said, "What! How can that be?"

I answered, "You can be rich in your heart."

He pondered the reality of my statement and probably still trying to figure it out.

*****

I had a license plate frame with "Millionaire In Training" etched on it and it got everyone's attention.

Then years later, I worked at a seminar with Ben's company which hosted other millionaires. It was called *Millionaires In Training*. They all had individual ways in which they made their fortunes and shared the stories with the audience. Afterward, I was speaking with a lady, who was inspired by my charisma and bubbly personality.

She said, "*You* should be a millionaire."

I said, "Oh, but I am."

She was then embarrassed by her comments, so I explained. "I am so abundantly blessed by life, my heart is overflowing with wealth."

Tears came to her eyes, as she knew my statement was true.

*****

I went to a workshop a while back and we all had name badges. I took mine off when we continued on to the reception.

My friend said, "You should leave that on, how will people know you?" I had to laugh, people always remember me. And I hope what they remembered about me didn't embarrass me too badly.

*****

I was on a cruise ship and was in the shower, when they started the fire drill. They were timing it and had to wait for all passengers to be accounted for. The person in charge of the drill had the cabin staff knock on my door, and then, they came in. To prove their ship's efficiency, they scurried to help me get dressed as quickly as possible, and I was laughing so hard by the time they fastened my life jacket. I ran up to the top deck, trying to sneak in formation without being noticed.

One of the passengers asked me later, "Weren't you the one in the shower?"

*****

A lady kept staring at me and it was making me uneasy.
Finally she said, "Where did you get those beautiful blue eyes?"
I thanked her and quipped, "They came with the face!"

*****

Alan, my son, was in elementary school and his class earned a special treat. The teacher was taking all the children on a walking field trip to get ice cream cones. The store was about a mile from the school and there were about thirty kids.

I asked my son, "Who is helping the teacher with the trip?"

He said, "No one."

I told him. "Tell your teacher I will help out."

A frown came to his face and he said, "Mom, I don't want you to go."

I was stunned; the kid was always in tow and he had never said that before. I volunteered regularly at the school and was his den leader in Scouts and team mom in sports. What could possibly bring about this request?

I imagined everything, and hesitantly asked, "Why don't you want me to go?"

He responded, "Because if you go, you won't let me have three scoops of ice cream!"

*****

Alan was the hero of the house. One day he just arrived home from school and I was on my way home from work, when two robbers broke into our house through the backyard window. He heard the ruckus and they were going from the bedroom toward the front room.

He ran to the front door and quietly opened it and then slammed it shut and yelled out, "Freeze, police." The would-be bandits turned and ran back down the hall and jumped out the window, never to return to this house.

*****

I lived on a lake when Alan was little and he never had any fear of water. He would run to the edge of the lake and just drop in. He taught his sister how to swim, when many lessons failed. Water was his test for everything, even brand-new shoes. If it flushed or floated, it passed the test. He had one lesson and he could swim!

We were on a very tight budget and I did a variety of jobs to make a living. I cleaned motel rooms and dug up peanuts for the farmers and Alan was always close by. We had a rowboat and went fishing every day. We had fun and he never knew it was our main source of dinner. His great-grandma lived nearby and was happy when we moved closer to her.

When I was having a bad day and life felt like a shipwreck, my evening work schedule allowed me to go to the beach almost every day. I would sit in the sand and float off into a daydream about life and love and any problems vanished out to sea immediately, as the soothing tide ran across my bare feet. It felt comforting like that again. We all enjoyed this life.

On Thanksgiving, the people of the town gave the poor families turkey dinners with all the fixins'. I had helped in previous years, gathering food for the needy and homeless and would certainly volunteer to help now. They came to my door, not to ask for my assistance, but to bring us the turkey. I was overwhelmed with emotion because I never thought *we* were poor, and that day I knew I was very rich, indeed.

I lost contact with Alan's grandma and great-grandma over the years. But imagine my surprise when I went the cemetery years later to visit my mom, and saw a headstone with a name that I recognized. It was only a few spaces down from my mom's. These people, who were significant in my life, and never met one another, were buried within a few feet of each other, in a cemetery that had 280,000 graves.

Alan's *three* grandmas were right there. It was my mother, his dad's mother, and his great-grandma. How *awed* is that!

*****

My friend had a large black lab dog, who was afraid of her little streetwise cat. The dog walked out of her way to avoid the cat. We were having dinner and everyone was passing bites to the cat. When the dog came to the table, they yelled at her to lay down and stop begging. The dog always obeyed, but not then. She stepped back but had such a sad look, as if saying, "This isn't fair, why is the cat allowed to beg?"

I got up and cut a piece of steak and fed it to her. Later, she came up and nudged my elbow and licked my arm. I glanced down and patted her head. (Good doggie.) She "purposefully" did it again and I looked into her eyes, which seemed to say, "Thank you." I smiled at Margy and my eyes told her, "You're welcome," and she was happy and laid down in her bed.

*****

I was driving a U-haul truck by myself, moving my belongings to Utah. I was low on gas and had no idea how far I could travel, as "E" was becoming a neon light. I had driven that road probably a hundred times and knew a town was about fifteen miles away, but could I make it? I really needed to find a gas station, but I had never remembered seeing one before the next city. All of a sudden, I noticed a small and all but hidden town, with nothing visible except one gas station. It was the town of Harmony. I laughed and gave thanks. Yep, the universe *is* in harmony.

*****

I am routinely inspired and often in awe, as I drive. It's a real source of calm and freedom for me, and the most unusual things seem to happen. If I get a flat on a long and desolate highway, someone immediately drives up and changes it in minutes. When I need to put on snow chains, someone stops and puts them on for me, or says the snow is only bad for a few miles, let me hook you up to my tow chain and pull you up and over this hill.

*****

I had been driving a company car and got caught in a flash flood. There's something about water up to your windows and mud flushing through the engine, which changes the whole life of that vehicle. I called my boss and he agreed to let me use a pickup truck temporarily while they tried to repair the car. I was driving, and I spotted what appeared to be my front truck tire passing me on the freeway. I tried to make my way off the road as the truck started to shake. When I got to the side, the truck tipped over due to its broken axle, and a stranger pulled right over.

"Do you need to use my phone?" he asked.

I was almost afraid to call my boss with this unpleasant news. I was bewildered by this run of bad luck I was having. Maybe I should tell him in person.

I was attempting to explain, "I'm trying…"

He smiled and said, "Yes, you are *very* trying!"

*****

I worked with hospice patients. These people were generally on their last leg and most were bedridden.

I always asked these patients, "What can I do for you? What one thing would you really like?"

It might be their last request to go somewhere (like the mall, for all the chocolate they could eat) or see something they enjoyed (like a play). It could be just a passing fancy, like a special meal. Whatever it was, I tried to make it happen. One lady wanted to see all of her adult children who were scattered everywhere, before the cancer took her. I rounded up most of them and what a reunion! Her heart was filled with joy and that carried her all the way to the end.

The next fellow had a lifelong dream to dance at the ballroom on Catalina Island. He met his second wife at a friend's wedding and they danced together all night and it was love at first sight. They were married over twenty years. His birthday was coming up and it was going to be his last. I used hotel gift vouchers and frequent flyer points and made it happen. He bought fancy dance duds and he and his wife went off for a couple of carefree, "living the dream," days before he passed away a few months later. I love when a dream comes true!

There was the sweet Italian lady. I got her out of bed and put a cheery holiday outfit over her and took pictures and made Christmas cards for the family. She signed the cards, using every ounce of strength to make a squiggle. Her family cherished that gift from her.

I cared for a cute couple, in their eighties. She had Alzheimer's and liked to watch game shows, all day.

She asked me every few minutes, "Do you like game shows?"

Her husband was in hospice and was very ill and fading fast. He had owned a business in the city and I sat by his bed and we talked about that. Each time I visited, I took him *one* thing. It could be a banana or a Twinkie, maybe a piece of homemade fudge or miniature angel food cake. He couldn't wait to see what his next treat was.

All of a sudden, he announced, "I would like to get out of bed."

I was surprised and helped him up into the wheelchair.

The next week, he was rolling himself around the house.

His daughter who hired me, exclaimed, "What did you do to him? He acts like a young man and he's eating better. It's amazing!" He died a happy camper!

That scenario happened with many separate patients. It seemed so easy to me, the smallest thing, gave them new life and they lasted longer than the relatives and doctors expected. It was gratifying.

*****

I attended a workshop and we were given a rock and had to write one word on it that described us. I wrote *awedsome*.

The facilitator said, "Don't you mean *awesome*?"

I eagerly stated, "Nope, in this life, I am awed…some!"

Chapter 9

A boss I worked for several years ago bought me a T-shirt, and across the front were the words, "What Are the Odds?" It was becoming quite curious and comical.

He claimed, "I have never known anyone, except you, who has had as many strange and interesting things happen in their life."

Today I was laid off from my job. I saw the writing on the wall and hoped the ax wouldn't swing too far in my direction. The timing was very ironic, because I recently decided to take a part-time job to pay off some bills and do some of the things I didn't have time or money to do. Well, I got the news and wondered what I would do next? I wasn't prepared and had to create a backup plan, fast. I depended on that biweekly paycheck.

I called the agencies and got my resume together and went in for interviews for a permanent, here till you die, job.

I always tried to be honest and told them, "Accounting is not my career and it's not likely I will be here in five years."

The employer seemed a bit offended and inquired, "What *is* your career?"

I replied, "I'm good at accounting and just fall into that position because it comes easy, but I have other long-term plans for my life."

One employer said, "You have all the required experience, but no degree and you're so close. If you wanted to get your degree while you worked here, in another position, you could have that job."

Later on, I actually did take that other similar position but passed on the degree. It's funny, during the interview, to see their face scrunch up, in disbelief, to think I wanted a life outside of work.

I applied at a local ski resort for a large construction accounting position and after two hundred applicants applied, I was called in for an interview, and I came in second. I didn't mind not making the cut, but hearing the words "second place" was annoying.

Time out—I need to pause for a moment, while I add an insert to this story. I have to tell you what *just* happened. Look back at the previous paragraphs, where I used the word "scrunch," which is a rare choice of words for me. Well, as I was printing this page, one of many chapters that have sat dormant in my word processor, I needed to take a break from writing and turned on the television. The actor who owns *that* resort was on TV and one of his movies was playing.

You might say, "So what? That's just a coincidence?"

But the scene in the movie, was that actor playing Scrabble, and the word he spelled out was "scrunch." I did a double-take; yep, that was the word, and that was the actor, and that's the page I just printed. I wondered, *What makes it so? Why did I turn on the TV just then? And see that scene, just then? Not two or three chapters ago, or watching the movie for a while, but, just then?* It amazes me *every* time.

Okay, back to my other story, coming in second. I took my real estate license test in Arizona and just knew I passed it and reported that result to my boss. He had paid for my classes and expected me to be licensed to help with his business. But I was quickly discouraged when I was advised, I missed *one* question. The guidelines at that time were, even if you missed any questions, all of the classes had to be retaken, and then retake the test. Of course, shortly after that, the rules were changed to only take the class for the questions missed, not all the classes.

I was still on the job search. The first callback of the day, before I could leave my house with my joyful mood, was that, once again, I came in second for a job I was qualified for.

The interviewer said, "We will keep your resume and call you if this other person doesn't work out."

I wished they would just say, "We hired someone else."

Then I would never know how close I was. What a teaser… always close, but no cigar. I don't know if coming in second annoyed me more or it made me try harder?

I needed a game plan. I needed to be focused, confident, and trusting of this situation. So I paused and "remembered to breathe" and became aware of the things I believed, that were true for me. I decided to take the morning off to refocus, by listening to music, like Jan and Dean, Yanni, or anything else that fed my spirit, at that time. Then, after listening to some affirmations, I would recite some of them out loud. This process gave me a new perspective, especially when the day seemed to be going downhill real fast.

I started out like Robin Williams…Goood Mooorning, Paaatty!

Today is a beautiful day, my heart is filled with love and I will be the best I can be.

I look and feel wonderful today.

I am so blessed.

Thank you, God, for all the blessings of this brand-new day.

I am empowered with greatness on this exciting day and I bring about what I think about.

I am powerful and have total and complete control of my life.

I am grateful for each and every thing that happens to *and* for me.

I am responsible for attracting the right and perfect job, for my highest good.

I began to feel some motivation and scanned the newspaper and faxed my resume to several companies. The mood I fell into earlier was changing and I almost, if I squinted, recognized a light in the distance. I usually have a smile in close contact with my heart, and I can tell how bummed I am, by how long it takes for my foot to start tapping to the music.

I like music; it frees my mind to work on the solution. I allow myself to feel all the emotions that arise from any situation, but then, I move my feet and take the necessary steps to find that new job or, follow that dream.

Then, I was even more inspired when a business bonus check that had been held up, arrived in the mail, and this day that wasn't very pleasant in the beginning, was turning out perfectly.

A company called me after receiving my fax. I went in for an interview and he gave me the details of the job.

I was puzzled, "I think I made a mistake and faxed my resume to the wrong company. I don't have this type of experience."

He said, "Oh, I know that, but you seem to be the perfect fit and I believe you can learn the job, easily!"

I wanted to find a new job by choice and not from panic. I wrote out a specific affirmation for this situation. I had proved this worked for me, many times before and saved it for when I really needed it.

I wrote, "I DECLARE, with FULL INTENTION that I will be employed by the first of next month, on a delightfully improved job that will fulfill all my personal and financial needs. I *am* paid equal to my skills."

I dated and signed the note and displayed it where it could subliminally be seen daily, without being overly focused on it. Thanks for the tip, Og Mandino!

Also, my subconscious, and all those extra helpers out there in the universe, could work on the solution, as well.

My current boss called me and said, "I've decided you can stay here until you find another job." He was going to hire his son's girlfriend, but that didn't work out. That was a nice surprise and it gave me about a month to shop around for the right job.

But the call that really cracked me up, was from the employer I worked for, ten years ago, who bought me that funny T-shirt.

He said, "I know this is an odd call, and I'm only grasping at straws. But is there any way you can come back to work for me, even temporarily, to get me through a big mess?"

I had to laugh and told him, "You won't believe this, but I was just laid off from my job and I can do anything I want to do! When do you need me there?"

What Are The Odds?

Chapter 10

I SOLD MY BOAT AND really miss it. I loved the freedom it gave me and how the wind blew in my hair as the seagulls chased the boat looking for any kind of food that might be tossed to them. The marina ducks were at my slip whenever I arrived and waited as if glued to the dock until I returned with the possibility of snacks for them. Did you hear the one about the duck who went into the hardware store and asked, "Do you have any corn?"

The owner said, "No."

The duck went back the next day and asked, "Do you have any corn?"

The owner yelled at the duck, "No, and if you ask me that again, I will nail your feet to the floor."

The duck went in the next day and asked, "Do you have any nails?"

The man shouted, "NO!"

The duck said, "Then, do you have any corn?"

These ducks seemed to know my boating itinerary and were always there waiting when I returned.

When I moved, I left the boat in the marina in Arizona, and after a while, I couldn't justify the expense since I never went back to use it. I loved the "idea" of having a boat slip, even if I didn't own a boat. I used to watch the TV show *Quincy* and liked how he lived on his boat and would walk down the dock to get to his house on the water and thought, *I could do that*, in a heartbeat.

I managed a property for a well-known magazine photographer, who took pictures of woman all day and needed to get away. Mark found that statement hard to believe.

"Why does he need to get away? I would love to have his job."

Men! He was coming to the river, and I had his house leased out and suggested he stay at my condo since I would be out of town. He accepted my offer and brought a couple of buddies to enjoy the week of fishing, boating, skiing, and relaxing. His boat wasn't working and asked to borrow mine. I met him at the marina and had a long list of instructions for him to follow.

He looked at me and started to laugh and said, "Your house is worth ten times more than this boat and you handed over the keys without any instructions!"

When the photographer was leaving, I asked if he could stop by Mark's house and say hi. I went over there and waited for the surprise guest. The doorbell rang, and when Mark answered it, he was stunned. He recognized his face from the magazine and invited him in for a beer. Never in his wildest dreams did he expect that. Surprises are like birthdays, you got to have 'em!

I went to the river on weekends with my girlfriends and had my teenage son with me. He liked to wander around the beach and swim. We went dancing on Saturday night whenever we were there. We hung out on the beach, scouting for guys to take us dancing. I found a real cute Marine, and we started walking down the beach and making plans for the evening, when Alan spotted me and came running up.

He was hollering out, "Mom! Mom, wait up."

Why is it when you lose your children in the market and search everywhere, you can't find them, but when they need money or to borrow the car, or your clothes, they can always find you?

Jeni said I had to tell you this story. I love when our sweet children, who we love and nurture, are so supportive. A group of my co-workers came out to play on the lake for the weekend and brought all their water toys. We decided to go to the beach for a while and then grabbed a bite to eat and the children played on the beach until their food settled. Everyone was swimming and relaxing and enjoying the warm sun. I didn't float my boat on the rocky beach anymore, because it seemed like I was keeping the propeller shop in business. So we dropped anchor a short distance out and we all swam to shore.

When it was time to leave, I got my kids into the boat and all the others were in their boats already, waiting for me. Mark was behind me giving me a boost into the boat. I climbed in over the side, as everyone watched and to my shock, my bathing suit top caught on something and was torn off. Oh my god! I immediately dropped to the deck, trying to reassemble my clothes and save some dignity. My co-workers *and* my children were rolling on the deck, in hysterical laughter. I was so embarrassed and thought, I'll have to quit my job, now! I went back to work on Monday and tried to be incognito, as I went to my desk.

The guys spotted me and said, "Good to see you, again, Patty!"

Yep, I'll pick up the want ads on my way home.

What is the definition of the word, boat? "A big hole in the water that you throw money into." My friends and I were out on the lake, and it was such a beautiful day. The water was undisturbed and we decided it was the perfect fishing hole. My friend's dad asked me earlier, if he could throw out the anchor when we found the right spot.

Then, in anticipation, he said, "Can I throw out the anchor now?" and was at the ready to toss it out.

I looked back and said, "Okay, this looks like a good spot," and he tossed it overboard.

I really hoped when he did that, it would have been attached to anything *on* the boat. We all watched as the anchor quickly sank to the river bottom and the rope sort of waved to us, as it disappeared.

I was dating a guy named Dan and we planned a holiday getaway with our kids. We had never tried this before, but I expected this would be fun. My kids enjoyed camping. Some of our friends were coming and bringing their boat. I was working two jobs and we would all leave for the lake after my part time graveyard shift ended. I was driving my car, since it more reliable and spacious. I borrowed a very large canvas tent from my friend's dad and rented a camping stove. We had coolers of food that we could cook throughout the weekend to minimize the cost.

It was a long drive, and I was exhausted by the time we got there. We wanted to put up the tent first and get settled in before we started dinner. Just then, an enormous freak wind blew in off the lake and tore out the whole side of the tent. We were shocked. The blustery wind was pelting us with dirt and debris, so we moved our cars into a horseshoe shape to block us from the increasingly strong winds. We had enough protection from the cars and decided to start dinner.

It was a good thing we had all this cooler food available. A yummy cooked dinner would do the trick.

Then, the camp stove wouldn't work. Everyone tried to get it started, checking the propane and valves and knobs, but it was useless. We had to go into town and buy something to eat. The kids were tired and cranky—oh yeah, that was me!

We had no other sleeping arrangements at that point and tried to find a motel room and every place was sold out. Our friends had enough and headed home.

We decided we might be better off with that plan also.

The day was now night, and I hadn't slept in what felt like three days. Dan could drive us home, and I could get some sleep.

We were about two hours into the drive and my trustworthy car broke down. We coasted into the small town, but the garage was not open then. We had to stay in one motel room overnight. His kids were crying and throwing fits. They were too old to be such brats. I was really stressed with their endless whining (wished I had some cheese to go along with that whine!) and Dan was not doing anything to get a grip on his kids. I was pouring money out the window and soon would be pulling my hair out.

The next morning, the car was fixed and we hit the road. I was so happy to see Dan's street and I tried to slow down as I shoved them all out. What an experience! Camping is definitely the make or break of dating.

Jeni still tells the story, "Don't go camping with my mom, she will yell at you!"

I got closer to my house and saw a sign that advertised canvas tent repairs. Oh finally, some good luck! I felt bad that I ruined this tent that I borrowed and needed to get it fixed and the damaged tent was stuffed in the trunk for a quick escape.

I parked in front of my house and rushed in to call the tent guy.

He said, "If you come over right now, I can fix it for you. I have holiday plans tomorrow."

I ran out to my locked car, and it was gone! Someone had stolen my beautiful 1965 red Mustang. I dropped to the curb in total disbelief. What else could possibly go wrong this weekend?

Amazingly, my car was recovered a few days later. It was found only four blocks from my house, hidden in some trees, because it ran out of gas! It was totally stripped and the trunk was emptied of all camping gear and coolers filled with food. Everything was gone, except the tent!

A large group of us from church chipped in and rented a houseboat for a few days over the holiday, and we had several boats and jet skis. Someone actually brought their older houseboat to add to the mix, and we shared everything.

We arrived on Thursday and others were coming in on Friday and Saturday. We had a motorboat to go pick up the new arrivals across the lake. We were one big, happy family. The Lake Powell party animals had a "simply *maa vaa lous*" time. The weekend was delightful and exhilarating, as well as spiritually bonding.

We started by gathering all the "kids" on the houseboat, where we were greeted with lots of hugs and laughter. The ambiance was a cornucopia for the senses, and every day was a new adventure. We played games, boated, skied, told stories, sang around the campfire, and did some sightseeing. We had fabulous meals and even caught catfish with brownies. The weather was just right, except for Friday night when that horrendous rain and blasting sideways wind unexpectedly roared through like one of those "Dorothy" things. But no problem, we all just huddled together as if in one big sleeping bag. (Did I say we bonded?) The atmosphere was beyond description.

We all were so in tune with nature and God, and we didn't touch down until morning.

Everyone was in charge of something. I was in charge of firewood. Granted, in the middle of the desert at the peak of summertime, it wasn't remotely possible that we needed a fire. The hot, dry air was probably sufficient. One of the ladies was trying to embarrass me in front of the guys. (Like I ever need help with that!)

She said, "Why don't you tell the guys we need a fire?" Guessing they would think I was beyond nuts. I agreed to mention it and see what the response would be. I sat alone on the beach and waited for the grand bonfire to appear, and little by little, everything arrived. One guy brought the wood over, another dropped off the matches, someone else rounded up kindling, lawn chairs were plopped down, the people started gathering and presto, a fantastic bon fire. Guitarists strummed along with our loud voices that echoed in the night air, as we circled the fire.

Of course, the crowd of singing night owls had to sit quite a distance from the hot fire and the next night, we discovered tiki torches might work better, but we all had fun.

There were several available boys, and the single girls were in heaven. I get along well with guys and attract them frequently, which puzzled some of the real pretty girls. I only wanted to impress one guy, and they could have the rest. The group was playing volleyball, and I walked over to join in. The ball was hit out of bounds, so I ran to get it on my way into the game. The first thing I did was trip and fall on my face in the sand. Maybe he didn't notice? I got up as if I planned to do that and tossed the ball in and turned away to spit the sand out of my mouth. I stubbed my toe when I fell and it had the makings of a bad sprain and was already beginning to swell, so by the end of the evening, I could barely walk or get up and down the houseboat steps. The guys waited on me hand and toe! They brought me ice and a chair and propped my foot up and looked after me. This possible sprain did have some advantages.

The next day, I was back in the game. My face was getting sunburned and playing in the heat made it so hot and flushed. We rotated positions and this guy (my guy) was on the other side of the net standing in front of me.

He remarked, "Your face looks so hot, can I pour some water on it?"

"Why yes, thank you!"

We took a brief time out from the game, and he held my head back and poured cool water from his water bottle down my rosy cheeks. Woo, that was refreshing, and so sensual in many ways. The others started tossing water and the volleyball game was now wet and wild.

The next day, everyone was boating and skiing and taking turns with all the toys. I was standing on the houseboat and wasn't planning to go out on that boat trip. This was my opportunity to show off my nautical expertise in front of this guy, who was on the bow of the ski boat. I could untie their boat and look really cool as I sent them off. I was standing by the rail and went to untie the boat, and I don't know what happened, but I slid off the houseboat and through the smallest gate opening, the size of a doggy door, and fell into the water and wound up under their boat.

"Oh my god, I hope I'm dead because this will be terribly embarrassing."

I had tried to grab the rail on my way out of the houseboat and nearly yanked off my little finger. As if that would have really saved me or stopped the cannonball effect. I came up meekly, still holding the rope in my hands and handed it to him. I'll never forget the look of shock on his face.

"Are you okay?" he compassionately inquired.

"Yeah," I quietly answered. "I'm okay—just fine… You have a good time—see ya later…"

I suspected my body would be severely bruised, not even to mention my ego, in about five minutes.

I saw the same look on his face later as I was just standing peacefully, minding my own business, and I slipped down a muddy hill. Oh no, not again! I didn't even know I could do the splits, but I sure hoped my other leg was coming too. Good thing we never dated, I would have killed myself in short order!

I sure do miss my boat!

Chapter 11

I THINK WE ARE ALL here to learn certain things. We have been granted certain talents and our focus can be on one issue or many and lasting our whole lives, depending on what we have chosen. Among other things, I'm here to learn about my spiritual self, living life, dealing with death, forgiveness, and letting go. This allows the spirit to be free to move along and do the work at hand. It reminds me of a caterpillar that has been completely transformed and leaves their old, but familiar, secure life behind, flowing gently into a brand-new experience, without any fear of change. You never see that butterfly dragging around that old cocoon. It's a lesson for us all.

I kept journals for years, mainly to keep track of myself. They were filled with pages of stuff that included nonsense, what if's, seriousness, complaining and inspiring stories. I read through some of these books and thought, I don't need to hang on to the memory of how angry I was at so and so, a decade ago, or who did me wrong, or who I did wrong to, or who was at fault in that argument. I threw out those journals that I saved, just in case I wanted to recreate my old caterpillar. That old negative stuff represented who I was then, not who I am trying to become now. I needed to be present.

I attended meditation classes that taught me how to be still, be present, and quiet my thoughts, but it was hard for me. I might not have had anything on my mind in the first place, but the second I was instructed to quiet my mind, everything ran through it like a car race. I sat quietly watching the track, I focused on the track, and the next instant, I jumped into the racecar and took off around the track. My mind was filled with any random thought. Did I pay the water bill? Wonder where Joe from high school is? Will that purse I bought match those shoes? My mind was like Elvis…it was everywhere!

It was helpful for me to create my own harmonious meditation space, in my mind's eye, where I could center, relax, and be present. I also made myself a meditation tape. Quieting the mind and turning off all the surrounding activity, even for a short time was so important and revitalizing.

I took several deep breaths, and sat comfortably, as I found my quiet place. I closed my eyes and visualized taking a long walk, down a secluded beach. I felt every grain of sand on my bare feet, as the warm sun embraced my face. I heard the waves gently brushing upon the shore and I paused for a moment to hear the message of the water, as it called me closer.

I took another deep breath, as I sensed my special place was close and I continued to walk along the water's edge. It was just around those uniquely chiseled rocks. A pristine lighthouse towered in the distance. My strolling steps became quicker, as I was being welcomed home.

The tall, pearly white lighthouse stood alone in the ocean air. The sides of the winding path that guided me toward the entrance overflowed with a variety of shrubs and foliage. Nearby were beautiful gardens with a multitude of flowers that were never out of bloom. The colors and fragrances teased all my senses.

I noticed a marble bench amongst the greenery that beckoned me, "Come sit for a spell," it seemed to say, "*Be* in this moment, right now." After a delightful rest, I casually entered the front door. The radiant light beamed through all the surrounding windows. I was completely present in *my* lighthouse.

I glanced around the spacious room that was bare of any furniture or fancy decorations. There was a lonely, grand piano in the middle of the room, a cozy rug in front of the fireplace, and a hammock hanging gracefully in the corner. It was a very comforting space and as I laid in the swaying hammock, someone played the piano softly, and I heard each note with a renewed clarity. I was connected and in tune with everything, as I meditated.

I liked being alone with myself, to get to know myself better. I believe we should be our own best friend and since we spend so much time together, liking ourselves should be a top priority.

Whenever I was on overload and my emotional bags were packed with stress, grief, loneliness, anger, doubt or fear, I was allowed to sneak off any time and visit this peaceful place, but always to return to my real environment, rejuvenated, and inspired. I had my trunk of stuff with me and with each step, the load got lighter. Once inside, I floated up to the highest window, where the beacon continuously lit the way, opened it and tossed the contents out. I watched all my cares and worries dissipate in the gentle breeze. I lingered a while longer and then leisurely strolled back home. The trunk was now just a tote bag and I was free to run and skip through the garden, down the path, around the rocks, and back to the beach. I arrived back home with a brand-new sense of self and purpose.

I love a sense of purpose. I met Elise West who plays the piano exquisitely.

Her words inspired me, "I can remember being two years old and trying to get on the piano bench to play."

It has been her passion her whole life. She shared this incredible talent every Monday night at the Cancer Wellness House in Salt Lake City, which was a safe, comfortable, and supportive place for cancer patients and survivors to visit. Her CDs were fabulous and her music took us on a journey to a faraway place where there was no pain or troubles. I watched as the audience was captivated to their very soul. What a blessing she was, as well as those whose passion *was* the Cancer Wellness House.

Where does that preconceived passion and talent come from? I think we bring it with us from lots of other experiences. My life is encompassed by passion, and it covers many different experiences. I have new beginnings all the time. I run into amazing situations every day and then they're gone, and the next project or adventure starts again. So I don't have time to savior and mull over every event, which I suppose makes every moment more important to me.

I was thinking about marrying this nice, dependable man, who I dated for quite a while, but he didn't have any passion. He didn't knock my socks off and vice versa. It was fine with him to let life decide everything, while I needed to participate.

My relatives said, "What's wrong with that? He's a decent guy, it doesn't matter." The words hung in the air, "It doesn't matter."

But to me, passion, participation, loving, and living a full life *has* to matter.

Chapter 12

It seemed like I had more than my share of death, and sadness. Some days were overwhelming, but then meditation kept me anchored, balanced, and centered. It taught me self-awareness, forgiveness, as well as letting go, which seemed to be exceptionally hard sometimes. My next prominent experience with death was when I was in junior high and my grandma Regina died. Aunt Jean seemed to be the family bearer of bad news. She was the one who had to call my parents because she knew I would want to know and maybe I would be able to go to her funeral. After the adoption, I wasn't allowed to visit my real family anymore. But I was allowed to go to my grandma's funeral.

Leota informed me, "This is last time you can see them. You live at our house now. They are not your family."

I loved Grandma Regina. She was the epitome of what a grandma is supposed to be, and I loved how she loved my mom. I enjoyed visiting her and she doted on me and we laughed and played. She took me to the park and we fed the ducks. We wandered around for hours, it seemed, and she held my hand and we talked and giggled about nothing. I used to play at the bottom of her back steps with a little doll she bought for me. I don't remember the inside of Grandma's house, or the neighborhood, but I always remembered the old wooden steps with the rickety handrail, where I played with my doll. It just felt nice whenever I was out there.

My favorite thing (besides Aunt Jean) was playing with my dolls. Aunt Jean always sent me Barbie doll clothes that she had made. I admired the tiny sewn details of each outfit. My grandpa Byron (my dad's dad) always made me doll furniture. These small things always made me so happy!

I stood in front of her casket, not knowing what to feel. I missed her, but this wasn't such a sense of loss, like it was before. Leota pulled my hand and made me touch her. Yikes. She was hard and cold and her spirit was really gone. I wondered, where did she go? What was the next step on this journey? I was more curious than afraid. My mom had a large family and everyone was gathered around to say goodbye. I don't know how their names were decided, but they were Jean, Joyce, Jerry, Johnny, James, Judy, Jill, Jessica, and Jennifer!

I said under my breath, "Oh, please take me home with you, Aunt Jean."

But I had been silenced when I was ten and wasn't allowed to express those words out loud.

My son had a class field trip to Sacramento to see the capitol, and Aunt Jean met us there to take the tour also. I routinely introduced her as Aunt Jean, as if it her first and last name!

She would tell them, "You can just call me Jean." Funny, the memories we keep.

It also reminded me of the time I said something to my dad, "Dad, can you...," and Mary started laughing.

I frowned at her and said, "Why are you laughing?"

She smirked, "You called him 'Dad' and you can't do that anymore." I could have pinched her good.

Grandma had saved a shoebox just for me in case we ever got to see each other again and my aunt gave it to me. Inside, was a faded old yellow dress, with a black and white photo of me and my grandma in the park. I was wearing that fancy dress and my hair was askew from chasing the ducks. I looked like a ragamuffin tomboy and the picture and memories were beyond beautiful. She also left me a lace tablecloth that I thought was so pretty and I still put it on my table during the holidays. She wanted me to always remember, even though life seemed unfair at times, especially with my mom being so sick, life was full of wonderful things. I love you, Grandma, thank you for what you gave to my heart.

I really missed my two aunts, Jean and Joyce. After I had my son, I went up to visit them. We went into the city to window shop and Joyce walked into a little shop and came out with a present for me. We never exchanged gifts and I was quite puzzled. She bought me a wonderful pink sand castle that played, "When You Wish Upon A Star."

"This is so lovely, but what's the occasion?"

She replied, "When I saw it, a while back, I thought of you, because of all the nieces and nephews and grandkids, you were always the one wishing on a star."

Star light, star bright, first star I see tonight, wish I may, wish I might, have this wish, I wish tonight. Yep, I guess I still do that!

I lived in Southern California and would visit Aunt Jean in Northern California, out of the blue, whenever I was in the mood. She had crocheted a special afghan for me and had a lemon meringue pie waiting for me whenever she knew I was stopping by.

She told me, "When you were little, you always loved my lemon pies."

She was the first one to read my book and liked it.

All these memories will stay with me forever. By coincidence, I happened to go to her house one day and she wasn't home. I called her kids to see if she was with them.

Jill said, "She is in the hospital, and is going to die today." I rushed over and got to visit and say goodbye.

Jill was astounded that I just showed up that day. "That is so weird you came today. No one knew today would be her last day." Coincidence, I think not!

The next death came just after I graduated from high school and my very best friend on the planet was killed in a car accident. I loved Wayne and we were so close for many years. We lived in a mobile home park, and he lived a few doors down from me. He smuggled me in yummy ice cream when I had my tonsils out and sat on the end on my bed and made me laugh when the appendix went. I went to his house and cried when things couldn't get any worse. He never judged the situation but hugged me, and then we ran off to play baseball. His mom taught me how to sew and treated me like a daughter. Wayne and I did just about everything together, in our youth. Sure, I'll climb over the city pool fence at night and go swimming with you. Yes, I'll write a note for you to ditch school. When his mom found out I wrote his note, she was so disappointed in me, she didn't speak to me for over two years. I was crushed.

So when Wayne died, I went to her door with a huge lump in my throat, not knowing if I was welcome even then, and we hugged and cried for what felt like an eternity. She knew how much I loved Wayne and how hard this was going to be for me.

I was running off to get married (I thought), and Wayne joined the Army. He came by my house after boot camp and looked so handsome in his uniform. We briefly "made out"! We were never romantically involved and never dated each other and I even went to my senior prom with his older brother. But we were connected in many other ways. He was always there for me; he was always my best friend.

I could feel something in the air that day. I knew something horrible had just happened. I couldn't explain it, but it was a nauseating feeling. A little while later, Leota came by my house. I had moved out on my eighteenth birthday! I thought I'm just not in the mood for her today. We fought all the time, and she never had anything nice to say.

She told me, "Something has happened, Wayne was in an accident." She was more compassionate than I had ever seen before. This wasn't good.

"What happened, is he okay?" I asked.

She said, "A lady stopped short in front of him on his motorcycle, and he went through her back window"—she paused—"he would have been okay, but when she looked back and saw him, it startled her, and she hit the gas and the glass cut his throat and he died instantly."

I couldn't believe it. I sat down and cried, "Oh my god, no, not Wayne."

Who would I play with now? Who could I share with? Who would I tell my secrets to? Who would laugh with me? Not my

Wayne anymore. I was devastated again and relived every emotion from my mom's death.

Wayne's spirit came and sat with me throughout the night. I could "feel" his crystal clear energy, sitting beside me.

He said," I will always be with you. Things are just fine." I cried and cried but felt surprisingly at peace. I knew without a doubt he was there that night, and I knew what he said was true. But when would this be fine?

Chapter 13

I HAVE A KNACK FOR finding things. I rarely lose anything permanently, and when it is lost, I can sense where it is. One day, an important file was missing in the office, and it was needed then. I stopped what I was doing and immediately began searching. I "felt" it was in the filing cabinet. I went through the cabinets, scanning every file and reading every label.

Another lady had filed it away and she couldn't find it either. But my feeling was so strong, I believed it had to be there. The other office workers looked around and they couldn't find it.

This funny (but useful) talent I have reminds me of that game when something is hidden and they say colder, warmer, or hotter as you get closer. I knew it was there, but what was I missing? I needed to ask my LAFF—that's my *Lost and Found Fairy*—to help me and to show me where to look.

In an instant, the idea came, "Look backward." That seemed sort of unusual, but I followed my guidance. I started at the letter Z and checked every file, looking from the back of each folder, so I couldn't see the labels, and there it was. It had been filed backward, and since the label was not visible, it might not have ever been found, since it blended with the other files. Everyone was quite amazed.

I joined several co-workers for a business lunch and one fellow lost his day planner. It seemed funny to me then how some people kept their whole life only in their planners and nowhere else. He was frantic because of the valuable information he had stored in it. The co-workers were trying not to panic.

I was calm and said, "We need to backtrack."

We checked in the restaurant, cars, trash cans, and walkways.

He nervously said, "What if someone stole it?"

I could sense it was only misplaced and not stolen, and it felt like it was around his car, and we kept searching.

You should see the funny looks I get when I say, "I can feel it."

They look at me with puzzled faces and ask, "What does that mean?"

"I can't explain it, it just works."

Again I ask, my LAFF, "Show me where to look, because Robert really needs to find his planner."

I ask for help but also give a reason why it needs to be found, it speeds up the process!

I opened his Suburban truck door and leaned down just a little bit and a black shadow appeared from under the seat where he had already looked three times. It had fallen down the side of the seat and slid way back and blended in, and with the light, just then, it was visible.

When the item is found, or I find the closest parking space at the busy airport, or catch all the green lights, or have the exact amount of money needed, as I dig through my purse at the store, I immediately say "Thank you" to that mysterious but expected source. TYG (Thank you, God) or TYLAFF. The more aware and thankful I am, the more it happens.

I worked in a convenience store to make extra money. I would have a little "saying of the day" on the counter. The regulars looked forward to seeing me on the weekends.

They teased and said, "Wow, we can get gas, treats, and affirmations here!" A nice-looking guy came in and bought candy for his Sunday school class. I counted the little candies and put them in a bag and smiled at him.

I exclaimed, "Thank you, have a glorious day."

He looked up and acknowledged my words and smiled back as he walked out the door.

Another guy who was in the store said, "Do you know who that was? That was Steve Young!"

I still didn't know who he was.

He continued, "He's a football player with San Francisco 49ers, and Utah's hero."

I guess I was supposed to be impressed, but not being much of a football fan, I thought he seemed like a nice guy.

A customer left the store and came right back in.

He shouted, "I lost my keys."

I responded, "Well, they couldn't have gone too far."

He searched everywhere and his buddies helped. He was carrying on and thought someone had stolen his keys.

I said, "Most likely if someone was in the mood to steal something, they might take the truck that the keys were attached to!"

I watched him come in and go out and search again and he was in quite a dither.

I said, "I *feel* the keys are inside your truck." Of course, he looked at me like I was nuts. (And that's why I don't run around saying that too often!)

He had a locking gas cap and said, "Maybe I locked the keys in there."

Besides the fact you needed the keys to lock it!

It was getting annoying as he asked me again, "Are you sure *you* haven't seen my keys?" Well, he *did* ask.

I remarked, "Trust me on this one, I have this talent of finding things and your keys are *in* your truck."

I didn't "see" his keys, but asked my LAFF, "Show me where to look, this young guy is going to have an attack if he doesn't find his keys."

I heard my inner voice say, "In the truck, between the front seats."

I told him, "Go out and look once more, look between the front seats."

He was beside himself. Then, he was driven to prove me wrong and would look one last time.

He came in with a big smile, almost laughing in disbelief. He said, "I found my keys, they were lodged between the seats and when I stuck my hand down by the gearshift, I felt them!"

His friend, who was calling for help, hung up the phone and exclaimed, "You said they were in there!"

"Ahh, no biggie."

I thanked my lost-and-found fairy and smiled as they drove off, recounting the story.

The other customer commented, "Now that *was* as impressive as Steve Young!"

The key ordeal reminded me of Mary. She was scattered to the wind, as usual, while she gathered her children together for our family outing. I was the timekeeper with a scheduled itinerary to make sure she was back home in time for her other plans. She locked her keys in the house and was going into this same dither thing.

I shook my head and said, "Since I am driving, it doesn't matter if you have your keys now or not, they will still be locked in the house when we get back, and by then, your husband will be home and I bet he might even let you in!"

Another customer came in and the computer at the pump couldn't read the magnetic strip on his credit card. He looked bewildered by having a bad credit card.

I told him, "I had a bad credit card like that once, but I put it in the corner, and now it's better."

He started cracking up, "You sure missed your calling. You should be a comedian."

I love what a smile does for a face.

It was an interesting process looking through my old journals. It gave me a chance to see where I was, how my ideas and dreams manifested, and what steps I took to get to where I needed to go. I realized that on many occasions, I limited my own prosperity. When I learned to listen and trust my inner guidance, I could see with peripheral vision and not with blinders. I saw things develop that I was basically testing a theory on, and now I know, they *do* work. I've seen magical things happen, in ways I would have never dreamed of.

I woke up to a song in my mind, "*Take me out to the ballgame.*" I thought that was a funny tune to be singing in the morning. I turned on the TV shortly afterward and they were doing a news story on baseball fields and the crowd was singing, what else but...*take me out to the ballgame...*

I wake up to music every morning and not coming from the alarm clock, since I rarely set it. I have a built-in alarm system. Before

I fall asleep, I call in my schedule to the *Timekeeper Fairy*. I always call these little helpers fairies because I can't explain them tangibly.

I say, "Please wake me up at this certain time," and every day, without fail, a song or music starts playing in my head that wakes me up at the exact time, or just a moment before. *Who put the Bopp in the Bopp Shoo Bopp…*or "*Getting to know you…*"

It could be Vivaldi or spiritual music, but every day, it's a different tune, with no rhyme or reason to the selection, but I sure do appreciate it. If I really need a wakeup call, maybe from a power nap or to catch an early plane, I ask to be woken up just before the alarm goes off, and it works every time.

To turn off my interior alarm, I simply say, "Thanks," and the tune in gone.

I believe everyone has these capabilities and it is a matter of listening and knowing it's possible. I was talking to a guy who had heard a few of my stories through the grapevine and said he was trying to listen to his inner guide.

He wanted to know, "What do you hear?"

"Hmm, what do I 'hear'? It's not actually audible, so much as an intuition or a knowing. For example, if I lose something, I ask, where should I look and a picture will come into my mind's eye or a thought. The message is just there, without sound or words."

It's A Miracle Center in Salt Lake sponsors a retreat every August, and due to my work schedule, I can only go one or two days out of that week. They have different speakers and workshops throughout the week.

I ask for inner guidance, "Which day should I attend, that would be more beneficial to my spiritual growth?"

I feel my spiritual health covers a lot of areas and can come from an amazing or inspiring or just plain fun class. Maybe I need to connect with a certain person or issue.

This particular year, I inquired, "What day should I go?" I heard, not in a verbal voice, but if spoken without words. (I'm trying to explain how this works for me, so it makes some sense.)

"Wednesday."

Okay, I'll go to Wednesday's class. I checked out the schedule and one of the speakers was Jon Mundy, who wrote a book on listening to your inner guide. I thought, the powers that be must not have seen the schedule because Jon is speaking on Tuesday. I signed up for Tuesday's class, because surely that was the class I needed to attend. I paid the money and was satisfied with my choice.

I heard, as if louder, "*Wednesday*, you need to go to Wednesday's class." I almost laughed out loud and immediately changed the date and went to the correct class.

I happened to get there as breakfast was being served and was seated next to Jon Mundy. How funny was that? I told him my story and he was amused. The class I went to was the perfect class and it was clear I was supposed to be there, that day.

I was driving home from a weekend getaway and was running low on gas and time. I suspected I could make it home and wasn't real concerned. I heard, "Go to that gas station." I noticed the station ahead and looked down at the gauge and thought, *Naw, I can make it home.* The feeling intensified, and I heard, "Get off the freeway, now." Okay, I will! I changed lanes quickly and barely made the off ramp and went to that specific gas station, and it was closed. I was annoyed, now what was *that* for? I had to circle back clear through town to get back on the freeway.

I told a friend of mine of this strange ordeal. "Maybe you were directed to get off the freeway to free up space for a preventable accident and knowing you would listen, you were told," she said.

I never told her my boat story of years ago, but the thought was there, and I knew what would have happened if I was pulling my boat that day. I really believed what she said could be true.

I was doing my sales job and was staying at my cabin in the mountains. I was in a lazy mood because it was such a lovely day. I dragged my feet for weeks to get up to the area where more sales were likely. I procrastinated long enough and made myself get up and get going. The drive wasn't far but the winding roads were a nuisance. It would be a full days project, but it would be enjoyable having lunch there.

I was about ten minutes into the drive and I heard, "Go home." I thought, *Now that's ridiculous.* It took everything I had to make myself go up there today in the first place. I kept driving. The words seemed louder, "GO HOME." I'm not going home, I am going to work up the hill. (No, I'm not having a meltdown. I'm just talking to myself!) I started to get serious stomach cramps and realized, *Maybe I should go home?* There must be more to this message than I'm paying attention to. I got home and my cabin was filled with gas as thick as fog. I hurried to shut it off and called the gas company and he rushed right out.

He fixed the problem and exclaimed, "Boy, are you lucky you came home when you did, with this much gas accumulated and the pilot on, this cabin would have blown up in ten minutes."

Thank you, God.

I was going out of town with a friend, and I just moved to a new apartment complex and she was picking me up there. She was very prompt when we traveled and would probably come in to see the new place. I thought I would meet her downstairs, knowing that she will be ready to go and she can see my place when we get back.

She saw me standing out front and was surprised, "I was just thinking as I drove in, I wished you would be downstairs, I wasn't sure of the directions to your apartment."

Then at the motel, the next morning, I was laying on my bed writing and she was in the chair reading.

I said, "I bet you are ready for coffee."

She replied, "I was just, this very moment, thinking that. You sure are perceptive!"

I wondered who the perceptive one was; did she send out the subliminal message first, or did I hear the message first from the universe? She drinks decaf, so it wasn't like it was time for caffeine, and I don't drink coffee. I might have to ponder that idea. What comes first? It's like if I drive by some small furniture store and just then a commercial for that business comes on the radio.

I believe, the more we listen to our inner guidance and the message is coming from a source of good (or God), the more messages we can transmit, or receive, without interference.

Jeni and I were going to a good friend's wedding in another town. We casually drove along, and all of a sudden, cars started slamming on their brakes. My first reaction is always to hold my arm out in front of the passenger, even though they are in a seatbelt.

I looked in the rearview mirror and shouted, "Oh my god, oh my god."

My arm became rigid in front of Jeni.

She said afterward, "I wondered why you were overreacting like that. You had enough room and weren't going to hit anyone ahead. Boy, we were lucky!"

A car behind us in the distance had gone out of control and was swerving on and off the road and coming right at us. I needed to get off the road. It appeared he would hit us or jump the median and hit oncoming traffic. He had to stop, soon, but how? The car was picking up speed and was all over the road. He spun into the median and back out and was coming head on right toward us.

I yelled, "Oh no." I looked up to the sky and shouted, "STOP," and in that moment, in that *very* moment, his car stopped, facing backward in the grass divider and very close to our car.

Everyone watching was stunned. The four young adults were obviously shaken up but more amazed they had stopped that fast without an accident or damage to their car.

I rolled down my window and said, "Good job, guys, now if you turn your wheels this way, you can easily drive back onto the road."

The driver smiled, and they waved as they drove off and I guessed they were thanking their lucky stars for a long time.

We were on vacation and driving home from Utah.

Jeni had her learners permit and needed driving practice. We had more adventures with this luxurious LeBaron, and it did everything but tap dance. I pulled off to get gas and let her get behind the wheel. The car had electronic everything and drove like a breeze, so I didn't have any concerns. I buckled up and watched as she turned on her blinker and was aware of traffic. She had her foot on the brake and started the car. Then, the key locked in the ignition.

I told her, "Turn it off."

But the car wouldn't shut off. I went back into the station and got the mechanic and he couldn't turn it off either.

Of course, I asked my daughter, "What did *you* do?"

She snapped back, "I didn't do anything."

He said, "You can drive your car home, but if you need to stop, you'll have to disconnect the engine wires."

Oh, that's all I wanted, to be a mechanic. I didn't have much of a choice and wanted to get home.

I only had to stop once more for gas, so it shouldn't be that big of a problem. We stopped for gas and I unplugged the wires, then reattached them and we were on our way again.

We were about one hour from home and all of a sudden, I said, "I have to stop, I can barely keep my eyes open."

Jeni looked at me oddly, "What's up?"

She knew I would never spring for a motel room this close to home, and I didn't say duck down, because kids stay free, like I had done in the past.

I was overcome by the need to rest. Usually, when I get that close to home, I have no desire to stop anywhere, but to get home. This was a very strange exception. It wasn't late in the day, and I had driven this trip in one day, many times before. So the upcoming steep and winding mountain pass would have to wait until tomorrow and we would enjoy one more vacation day. We checked into the motel and there was a garage next door. I could have the mechanic fix the car in the morning.

The mechanic walked over and advised, "Oh, here's your problem, the wiring is bad, see how it's been causing sparks? But it has nothing to do with the key being stuck." Then, he turned the key and it came right out. "Hmm?" He continued, "Good thing you stopped when you did, you couldn't have driven even a half hour further, without having an engine fire and with the pass and this computerized electrical system, you probably wouldn't have been able to get out of the car in time."

I knew that statement was true because the alternator went out before, and in three seconds, nothing worked. The only thing I could say was "Thank you, God," in a *big* way.

I knew when it was time to write my book, I would be given beneficial clues and that day did come as the undeniable evidence mounted, in my favor. One of the many clues happened when I was moving and looking for something and grabbed a newspaper at the store. I blindly opened it to any page and saw the *big* headline: "Former resident's novel sold in local bookstores." Lake Havasu City resident published her first book, an inspirational novel and it's a big hit!

I added it to my "book affirmation" notebook that seemed to be growing rapidly, as proof was showing everywhere!

As far back as I can remember, I've been on a spiritual journey, and many years ago I saw a cute sheep dog and his eyes were covered with straggly hair and it reminded me of my life and I thought, if I ever write a book, I'll call it… So when I did write the book, I remembered the dog and the title, and maybe I could use that as my book cover?

I was visiting Sedona, Arizona, and I went into a metaphysical bookstore to buy a book and strangers all of a sudden were turning to look at me. I checked my clothes and face, in case I was wearing lunch, and thought, what's going on?

A lady came up to me, "You should have a picture taken of you aura."

It wasn't like they were having an aura sale and trying to drum up business. My intention was to buy a book and go home, but since I've never had this done, what the heck. A photographer took my picture.

When I saw my little face, about the size of a dime, in the middle of this big glow, I declared, "Wow, this *is* my book cover!"

She responded, "You are definitely on a spiritual path and this white area on your right is your spirit guide and the pink between you, is protection."

I showed the picture to my friend and travel buddy, who had witnessed some of the "awed" things.

I laughed and said, "Yep, my guides have worked overtime on me!"

She agreed and reminded me of our last excursion. We were going to visit another friend out of town and the weather was wintry but calm. I wasn't wearing my seatbelt and she expressed her concern. I knew she was right, but I still didn't fasten it. I assured her that I "know" if danger is close, and I did wear my seatbelt, just not every time.

We were about an hour and a half into the trip and I was driving at normal weather condition speed. All of a sudden, I "heard," "Put on your seatbelt and be aware." I reached for my seatbelt. The weather was still clear and she leaned over to help me fasten it, so I could keep my hands on the wheel. In an instant, the weather changed and it was snowing intensely. It felt like I hit black ice and the car began to slide and we were in a spin and all over the freeway.

I held my arm out in front of her and said loudly. "Hang on." I had no idea where we would land.

Pam had been in a horrendous car accident years ago. I subliminally told her, "Don't be afraid, now."

I put both hands on the wheel and turned into the spin and the active freeway was now clear, as we drove backward on the road at a speedy pace. It appeared we would be going off the embankment soon, and rolling could sure be the next option. The passenger door slammed into a metal mile marker that served as a buffer after leveling it, which also changed our direction and then, we were headed face down off the road and into the snowy, muddy ditch below. We came to a lopsided, but safe stop, as traffic above continued on.

We didn't roll and were both surprisingly calm.

She told me, "I wasn't afraid and watched what you were doing. I wanted to know how to control a skid and was going to take class on that."

Earlier, I grabbed a big handful of napkins from the convenience store and she was making fun of me.

"Did you get enough napkins?" But we used every one of them by the time we were back on the road. She had her cell phone and called Auto Club and people stopped to help. We were in good hands throughout the whole ordeal. The tow truck remained on the road above and winched us backward up the hill to the highway and there was no damage to us or the car, besides the mile marker imprint left on the door, and we simply drove off.

She was surprised, "I can't believe we are just driving away as if nothing happened."

And in moments, it was only a miraculous memory.

Thank you, guardian angels!

Chapter 14

BIRTHDAYS WERE FUN OCCASIONS AND every year my kids had wonderful parties. When they were little, we routinely gathered the neighborhood kids and went to the local pizza or ice cream parlor. As they got older, they could choose what they wanted to do for their birthday, and older still, we had to make them surprises because they wouldn't show up!

Alan loved his birthday, especially since it was in the summer. He liked to go to Disneyland, any other amusement area or Catalina, and could stay up as late as he wanted to watch TV. When he turned nine, I made him a clubhouse in the backyard. This was my first big building project. I thought it would take me about two weeks to build and keeping the kids away was the test. It turned out real neat, for a guy's fort! It was six feet by six feet. I put screens on the windows and a linoleum floor and made a Dutch door and hung up "macho" curtains. I started out with the two-by-fours in the corners and would assemble the reinforcement pieces as I went around the structure.

The first big wind that came along (five minutes later) blew it down, so I moved into the garage and built a wall at a time. Alan couldn't wait to show his friends and have them stay over in the rugged wilderness of the backyard.

I was handy with a hammer and a saw, thanks to my grandpa, who had a wood shop behind his house and made fabulous art carvings and furniture. I didn't read the directions, I just looked at the picture and could make anything, or create a new thing from what it was supposed to look like and I enjoyed doing interior home improvements.

I wanted a fireplace and made the appearance of one, in the living room. There was one wall that was perfect for creating that illusion. The path from the front door through the living room led to the kitchen. I had previously hung a set of swinging doors in the kitchen entryway, to separate it from the living room. If I had company and the dishes weren't done, I closed the doors.

I attached red z-brick pieces on the lower half of the wall to resemble the bottom of the chimney and added a marvelous oak mantle. I added a beautiful-veined glass mirror that covered the whole wall above the mantle. I installed a little hearth with logs, fake of course, and presto, there was the perfect fireplace. Afterward, I discovered one flaw. Even if I closed the swinging doors to hide the kitchen, which was *only* messy if company dropped in, they could look in the mirror and see the reflection over the doors, right into the kitchen.

Jeni wanted to hide out for her birthday. She knew I would do something to embarrass her. Like the time I took her out to a fancy dinner and had a singing telegram sent to her. The guy who delivered the telegram picked her up and danced her around the floor. When she turned twenty-one, I sent twenty-one huge balloons to her work. So later, she went skiing or took road trips, just to be away from any risk of embarrassment.

We routinely stopped off for pizza after the soccer games, so her thirteenth was easy. We said goodbye to everyone and no one followed us, and no one was at the pizza parlor, and nothing popped out of anywhere, so she believed she was off the hook. But then, the whole team appeared and after eating, a food fight ensued and even the coach was decorated in cake and pizza. This was one time I *did* have to clean up the mess and it was worth every moment.

Then, when she was a teen, I actually had the surprise party, at her work. I called her dad and grandparents and had everyone show up there for dinner and she was really surprised, and not embarrassed, this one time.

Mary got her family together on their birthdays and since she had made each cake for her ten children, over the years, I volunteered to give her a break when I was in town, which was a creative treat for me. I felt each one had to have a special cake to fit their personality, or their sweet tooth.

One got a large macadamia nut brownie, baked in a pizza pan and covered with lots of fruit, swirled with chocolate and whipped cream. The other had a peanut butter cheesecake (my favorite) that was so deliciously rich, it rotted your teeth just to walk past it. Then, I made a vanilla cake with smooth banana pudding as the frosting and banana chunks throughout. Some of the ideas were simple, like special cookies or a cherry cake. They never knew what to expect, but were delighted every time.

I clipped and saved coupons all year, just for their birthday ingredients. But Christmas was a different story. We traveled many years to Utah for Christmas and I went to a store, like Costco, and bought lots and lots of food and treats. They didn't have extra fresh fruit often, and it wasn't available in a bowl on the table, to freely take as a snack.

My kids got so many things from the relatives, and as they got older, I wanted them to appreciate Christmas for the true reason, also. After my divorce, the kids spent Christmas Eve with their dad's family, then onto the step mom's family. They had Christmas Day with me and my family.

Jeni and I went to the Salvation Army, on occasion, and helped serve meals to the homeless and we took little gifts and candy to the nursing homes, before we opened our presents, or traveled away. One older lady in the home, was lost and followed Jeni all around.

"Will you take me to my room?" she asked.

We walked around the hospital and delivered our treats to the residents and this little old lady kept showing up, following Jeni!

She said, "Can I go home with you?"

One season, we didn't have a car and were in a quandary how to get the Christmas tree home. Some holidays we decorated large plants and in Arizona, a huge cactus was decorated. So this year the kids wanted a real tree. We walked down to the tree lot to check out the situation and found a nice, tall tree that we liked. Now we needed to get it home. We put it in a shopping cart and went as far as we could take the basket and then had to carry it the rest of the way home ourselves.

We laughed and dropped the tree a number of times and had sap and pine needles all over us, and it became more of a comedy than an effort to get this tree home. People driving by took a second look as they observed this huge horizontal green thing with nothing visible but legs, being maneuvered down the street. We managed to get it home and up the stairs, but decorating would have to wait until we recovered, from the delivery process!

I think I was so fond of holidays because of my mom. I regretted that she never got to meet her grandchildren. After I had my son, the doctor said it was unlikely that I could get pregnant again. I wanted to have a child with my new husband, Dave. He wanted a house full of children. We tried and practiced, taking advantage of every appropriate time and location, but it just didn't happen. I knew, in the back of my mind, if I had several children, I would only have *one* daughter.

We finally decided to give up trying after a few years and I could have my career, and we could buy that big house, and be in *big* debt. It took both of our incomes to qualify for that house, but within two weeks, guess who was pregnant?

We were thrilled beyond belief. I didn't care that we didn't get that expensive house and after a while, we bought a nice three bedroom house with a den and family room, and a big backyard. It was more affordable on Dave's income and I could be a stay at home mom.

My friends gave me an early baby shower and things moved alone fine. I worked for a doctor, and every day, I listened to the baby's heartbeat.

I was giddy as I pressed the stethoscope to my belly.

Then one day, there was no sound. There was no heartbeat. Oh no, something was seriously wrong. Maybe this thing is broken and I reached for another.

I prayed, "God, if I am going to lose this baby, please make it, be *now*." I knew I would never make it through the loss of my baby later.

I lost *her* the next day. The doctor had to induce labor so the baby would come out relatively easy, and then, I just went home. It was a horrible experience and I was devastated. I had no baby to take home, and like a thief in the night, I felt like I was swindled.

I gave away every baby gift. I didn't want anything to remind me that there was going to be *no* baby in this house. I was very depressed. I felt in my heart, I would have one chance for a daughter and I just used it up.

Life drearily continued on. I was angry and sad and was making life miserable for Dave. Things progressively got worse and we separated for a while and then got back together.

Shortly afterward, I was pregnant again. Oh no, I was excited, but afraid and very superstitious. I didn't buy one baby thing, I didn't have a shower. I did everything I was supposed to do. I was always very healthy, except for my female parts and I knew the baby could just fall out, at any time. I was in a constant state of worry, throughout the pregnancy.

The date was approaching and I was becoming a wreck. The escrow just closed on the house and we were moving that weekend. My mother-in-law bought the baby a crib, which remained in the box.

About two weeks before the baby was born, I had a very reassuring dream, my baby would be a girl and born on this certain date, at this specific time, it weighed exactly this much and was this long. I had a preview of this beautiful, healthy baby and her name, was Christine. I was so hopeful.

The day before the date in the dream, I went into labor.

The doctor kept saying, "You aren't in labor, so go back home."

I did recognize labor and knew this baby was coming, but went back home, anyway. I had to go back to the hospital with the same symptoms and they finally kept me there, just in case. They put me in a room, without a bathroom, and were going to give me an enema. Are they insane? The doctor came in and saw that my name was not the usual American spelled name, like Smythe for Smith.

He asked the nurse, "Can she speak English?"

I could pass as apple pie; are you kidding me!

I snapped back, "Yes, I speak English and I also know sign language, want me to show you." I was quickly becoming in a bad mood. What a stupid doctor.

In the early morning hours, my water never broke, but the baby was practically waving, "Hey, Doctor, yoohoo, anyone out there?"

My doctor was in the shower getting ready his hectic day, but everyone else fell into their assigned roles and my sweet little, actually an eight-pounder, daughter was born on that specific date, at that exact time and looked identical to the baby in the dream.

Everything, was precisely as the dream had showed me, including NO! I don't want another ice chip, Dave. I had a special name already picked out and never thought of Christine, but that is her middle name now. The maternity area was full and I had to go back into the labor room after delivery and wait until a room was ready. I wasn't thrilled about that, after a full day and night of intense labor.

The doctor finally asked me an intelligent question, "Would you like a shot for pain or something for sleep?"

I smiled and said, "Sure, I'll take them both."

I had "rooming in." She was in a drawer in my room and I could play with her anytime or send her back to the nursery, just by pushing the drawer in. I sat up in bed and had her in my lap and people walking by couldn't see her and probably thought that poor lady is talking to herself. I smiled proudly as they passed by. When we brought our daughter home to our apartment, she slept in a cardboard box on the coffee table, pending the weekend move to our new house. Several of the upstairs neighbors could see down into our living room and volunteered cribs and baby supplies. I kindly thanked them and explained that escrow just closed on our house and we were moving this weekend and this little doll is all set! I took my brand new baby home from the hospital and WE went *shopping*!
THANK YOU, GOD—

I held up the cute dresses in front of her and let her visually, if that's possible, pick the one she liked. If she perked up at one dress over the other, I got that one. People watched me doing that and with surprised expressions would inquire, "How old is your baby?"

I was filled with joy and answered, "Four days old."

I gave my children choices, as well as consistent boundaries. The experience with my son was completely different. It seemed my children were opposite in every way. I went into two day labor with Alan, and it seemed to last forever and I didn't want any shots or drugs if I didn't really need any. Labor dragged on and on. Finally, the doctor was going to give me shot, in the back, for pain. I saw the needle that could serve as a knitting needle as well and thought, *Oh no, if they are just now giving me a shot, I might be labor for days.*

I inquired, "How much longer is this going to last?"

He said, "About twenty minutes."

I laughed and said, "If I only have twenty minutes, that's a walk in the park, I'll pass on the shot, thank you."

I was fully dilated and then, he was trying to scoot back up. My stomach looked like a caterpillar crawling as it moved up into an arch and then went down again. The nurses had to push on my stomach to direct him back down. Hey, bud, this ride is over. Keep your hands and arms inside the ride as you disembark!

They had to break my water and he immediately sailed out. I had my beautiful little boy (actually, over eight and a half pounds) during visiting hours and everyone was lined up to see the new addition. The nurses quickly cleaned him off and held him up in the nursery window for everyone to see. He wasn't fond on the outside world and let out a big yell.

The sever pains were gone instantly and they covered me up in a warm, from the oven, blanket, and rolled me into the hall to be with my family and friends and I felt like a million bucks.

My doctor was so amazed by my courage of having my first child, without yelling and screaming and begging for drugs, and considering how long and painful that ordeal was, he changed his practice and went into "natural" childbirth. What a concept!

I sat up in bed when I was nursing him and even when he was a few months old, I still fell asleep while feeding him. I would be jolted awake by his strange movement in my lap. He had slip down and moving his little head from side to side, as fast as he could, trying to catch the milk that was squirting all over his face!

When they were babies I made sure that no matter what time during the night they woke up and needed feeding or changing, I greeted them with a smile.

Jeni was learning to crawl and would come around the kitchen corner, drooling, and face covered in carpet fuzz, but always wearing a big smile.

They had chores and allowance from the very beginning and they knew what I expected. It didn't matter if they did them immediately (yeah, right!) or waited until five minutes before I got home, their chores were to be done. Alan put his toys away at the end of the day, as soon as he started walking, and Jeni did the same. They had their bedroom and play rooms, and toys stayed in these areas.

I wanted to be a good parent and knew what I needed to do. I was the parent, I made the rules and I showed them respect and courtesy, and they returned the favor. My rules, consequences, and love were always consistent.

I had three very important guidelines while raising my children. The first one was, I didn't discipline them when I was real angry, and sometimes that didn't work, but I really tried. I might have to count to a thousand, as they waited for me to calm down.

I told them, "If you have a problem or get into trouble, I would rather hear about it from you first."

Alan tested that theory more than once, like when he drove the neighbors car, without permission, and hit her house.

The second was, I cooked them a good, healthy breakfast every day to get them off to a good start.

I felt a box of cold cereal was as nutritious as the box itself.

Jeni had friends spend the night and warned them, "My mom will make you eat a real breakfast."

The third was, I wouldn't yell at them in the morning, but after school was a different story!

Jeni told me when Alan was watching her, and it was time to do their chores, he always made it fun, as she grumbled. He made up games, like how "fast" can you pick up your toys, or let's "hide" the dirty dishes in the dishwasher, or we can "squish" the clothes hamper monster with these dirty clothes. I appreciated him for doing things like that.

Then, there was the time I came home from work and kicked off my shoes before I walked into the kitchen, in my stocking feet. As soon as I hit the hardwood floor, I "skied" briskly across the room.

Alan was there to almost break my fall, and he was just beaming.

"What do you think, Mom?"

"What did you do?" I hesitantly asked.

"I waxed the floor for you."

I was assessing the damage and curiously asked, "What did you use?"

He proudly replied, "Pledge, furniture wax!"

Chapter 15

My four-year-old niece Ruby called me at nine thirty in the evening.

"What are you doing up so late?" I asked.

She said, "I don't have to go to bed until eight. I want to tell you a story."

Then, she said, "I love you."

I said, "I love you too, now go to bed."

She called me right back. Apparently, she just learned how to use the phone and found my phone number I had written down for Mary. I planned to pick her up on Saturday and she was double-checking my schedule.

She called on Sunday, "I just wanted to see what you were wearing to church."

I tried to spend a lot of time with the kids and brought them to my house often. They enjoyed just hanging out, and they would all be lined up on the couch. Once we rented five movies, at one time and they couldn't believe that. I made them dinner, of their choosing. They got to have seconds and even dessert. The youngest boy guarded his food and ate it close to his body, like a squirrel. Ruby liked to follow me, if I left the room to do laundry.

"What are you doing?" she inquired.

Apparently, I had an unfamiliar accent on some words.

I said, "I am worsching (washing) the clothes."

She giggled, "Worsch, worsch, worsch!"

I made her take a nap, on weekends, at a specific nap time. She wasn't used to a nap "time," or possibly even a nap at all. She didn't want to sleep when everyone else was up because she might miss out on something. I promised her, we wouldn't do anything without her. I put her in the spare bedroom and noticed her lying on the floor, her head peeking around the corner, just making sure, what I said was true. I picked up stuffed animals at garage sales and kept adding to her collection. She was happy and kept them neatly, on her bed, in her room. Once, I picked them up after dinnertime and Ruby said she was hungry.

I asked, "How can you be hungry, you just ate?"

She said, "I didn't have any dinner."

I called Mary up and asked her about that.

She said, "Oh, I guess I forgot to feed them."

My kids would never let me get away with that.

One child went to school wearing rain boots, in the snow, but no shoes or socks on underneath. Holy cow!

I had so much fun with her kids over the years and we went on many road trips together. I would mention I was going somewhere and by the time I got in the car, I had six children going also! One time, we were out for a short while and when we got home, Mary asked where we went.

I said, "We went to Las Vegas" (quite a distance from Salt Lake!)

She said, "That seems pretty far away."

I remarked, "But we drove fast!"

The kids still laugh about that.

My sister's children and I spent a lot of time together over the years. Previously, a couple of the kids came to stay with me during the summer and I gave them jobs in my office. Years later, I was invited to Alaska to help with the new arrival of my great niece. Unfortunately, I broke my arm, the day before leaving. Yes, same arm, three times! Fortunately, I couldn't change diapers, her husband cooked all the meals, I could only hold the baby, and if she cried, someone took her from my arms because of the cast. I was so pampered. Next time I visit a new baby, I'm renting a cast!

I am still closer to them, than with my sister.

Mary was divorced and was barely making ends meet, and even when she was married, they lived nearly in poverty. She could stretch a pound of hamburger into four meals for a family of twelve. Her husband was an unsupportive and abusive jerk, so good riddance. He threw one of the boys across the room and his son had to be in a body cast, for broken bones.

She went out dancing routinely, looking for a husband, and left the kids home alone. The older kids were able to care for the younger ones. I was surprised to hear she stayed out so late at night. She never kept track of them very well, and they would wander the neighborhood at all hours of the night. She met a man, who seemed like he would be a good provider and was planning to marry him. He had way too much baggage of his own and anyone with a brain, knew this was a mistake. This guy was trouble and you could smell it a mile away. How is he going to handle that many children? They were undisciplined now.

I tried to talk her out of it. "Wait a while before you remarry. You need to get to know this guy better and see how he interacts with your kids. He is *not* a responsible parent."

Mary was losing sight of reality and nothing was going to come between her marrying this guy. Her kids were ignored and had no supervision. She was basically dumping her children for this guy and I didn't approve one bit. I could hardly stand to be around him. Shortly after their wedding, we were having a family dinner and passing food around the table and he brushed up against my body with the bowl of mashed potatoes. My niece and I looked at each other. That sure wasn't an accident. I told Mary, he is not allowed at my house, ever, if she is not there. She just didn't it.

Her ex-husband decided he would take the five kids for a while and care for them. The other five were on their own, by then. She was so happy that he wanted to do this and give her some free time, she never thought twice about it. The number six child, just by chance, was staying at my house for a visit. She didn't go with her dad. But just for spite, he set up a tent, below a busy freeway off ramp, surrounded by some trees and left the three boys and their four-year-old sister there, alone. He went into town and rented a motel for himself.

The oldest of the boys tried to find their dad after three days. He hiked into town, not too far away, and stood on the corner, in the rain, as he looked around for his dad. The police saw him and took him back to the makeshift camp sight and gathered up all the kids and put them in the state's care. The oldest daughter, fortunately, happened to be at my house, or she would have been placed in foster care also, but she was too savvy to fall for that bizarre tent scheme in the first place. When there was a hearing, all that happened to that idiot dad was a slight reprimand and slap on the hand, not even any fine or jail time.

He told the judge, "I want to give up my parental rights."

Just like that, he was off the hook.

The courts took the kids away from Mary and blamed her for being a negligent parent. They said she couldn't care for them properly and the decisions she was making, wasn't for her children's welfare, but had put their safety in jeopardy, on several occasions. The three boys went into foster care, Ruby went to a relative of her dad's, and the oldest girl lived with me.

So only the memories of these sweet children made the wait for their questionable return a little easier. I would catch myself looking out for Ruby's face to peek around the corner. It was difficult to pack up the dolls and toys that were left behind on her bed.

They went to different homes and were allowed to visit me occasionally. I volunteered to pick them up at the foster family's house, an hour and a half away, and the foster dad would pick them back up, after visiting his mom, who lived close to my house. That worked out real well. The youngest nephew was at my house for the day, and I took a blanket out of the trunk.

I said, "I have to worsch (wash) this." He looked at me and grinned and mocked my words, like Ruby did. "Worsch, worsch, worsch!"

We both laughed and I was glad that even though he hadn't seen Ruby in three years, he had happy memories to hang on to. She was completely cut off from us.

I went to court with Mary and the judge and caseworkers asked if I could take her children, since we already had a good rapport. I had to really think hard and pray about that one. As much as I wanted to take the kids, I couldn't do it. I had raised my children and with my current job, there were times when I wouldn't be home. It bothered me when Mary left her children unattended in the past, to go on a date.

I couldn't start over with five children. I didn't have the finances or patience for that responsibility. Maybe, if I was married, I wouldn't have hesitated, but at that time in my life, I couldn't be the attentive guardian they needed.

Then the guilt came. "But they are family." I had lived all sides of *this* coin, and I had to make a very hard, but conscious choice, as I answered, "No, I can't take them."

Later on, Mary was diagnosed as bipolar, and her ex-husband's cousin agreed to take Ruby and care for her until the long court battle was settled. There were many issues to be resolved and Ruby was eventually adopted by them, while the other three remained in foster care, until they were eighteen.

Mary was very upset when she heard the ruling of the adoption. She felt it was unfair, and that the judge didn't like her. She tried in every way to get the ruling overturned, but she also knew the reason for the court's decision wouldn't change the results.

She said, "The judge doesn't trust me with my own children. I have to have supervised visits."

She asked me, "Can you testify in my behalf?"

I would help her in any way possible, but not with that request.

That *one* choice of picking that man over her own children, changed many lives and the damage would be long term.

I hated losing my family again, and I knew then what my dad's message meant.

Sometimes, as we go through life, we claim responsibility and guilt for other people's problems that aren't ours. It may come from children, parents, a relationship or siblings. It could be a boss or co-worker who asks us for something and we would rather not do it. But we feel guilty or afraid to say "No" and then by saying, "Yes", it makes our lives miserable. So then, not only do we have our stuff to deal with, but theirs as well, and if by magic, they are free. Where does that leave us? We are trapped *under* the guilt and worry wagon.

After several occasions with those type of experiences, I realized that doesn't work for me. We need to be individually responsible, as much as possible, for ourselves, for our choices, and for the consequences, *and* blessings that result from them.

I volunteered at church for a variety of events and they always knew if I didn't want to do something, or it wasn't "my thing," I would just say no. I didn't have to explain, or feel bad. One day it was snowing outside and the church administrator called to ask me if I wanted to do some special project and I was too busy then.

I said, "I can't because I'm mowing the grass." He paused for a moment and responded, but it's snowing outside."

I stated, "I know, but *all* excuses are equal!"

My son got injured in high school while rough-housing in the classroom. There was a scuffle and a kid socked him in the eye. I was angry as he tried to explain what happened and I didn't believe that he couldn't see. He didn't have a black eye or any pain or swelling and I had no idea how serious his injury was. I didn't take him to the doctor right away. When I did a few days later, they said his retina was torn and he had to have eye surgery immediately. I arranged my work hours to be at the hospital as much as possible following the surgery, which was daily, but not for long periods. I was a single parent, getting no child support and worked a long way from the hospital.

His eye was in a delicate state, and he had to have drops put in his eye throughout the days and had to lie on his face, so the blood could be absorbed.

Shortly afterward, the retina tore again and the doctor came in to talk to us and said, "The retina has detached again and we need to go back in right away."

There was no delay as I answered, "Schedule the surgery."

We love and protect our children and try to keep them safe from harm or bad days, but we just can't do everything.

Alan was angry with me. He said, "Thanks a lot, Mom."

The surgery was scheduled on his birthday...

And he had been laid up already with the previous surgery... and he couldn't play baseball anymore, in case he injured his other eye…and his dad was getting remarried…and she had two kids…and I wasn't at the hospital twenty-four hours a day, and on, and on.

Fortunately, we had good insurance.

I was on overload. The next few years were some very hard times.

He felt, *all* of this was my fault, and of course, I did too. Then, after seriously beating myself up and taking all the blame for everything in the world, it finally dawned on me. I didn't ruin his life, and I didn't hit him in the eye, and since none of that, in reality, was my fault, why was I racked with guilt?

There wasn't one thing I could have done to prevent or change any of it. He remained angry for years and then became estranged from us, and that's still a hard pill to swallow.

I never had a mentor or role model or any emotional support, and I had to make many choices based on my own values and belief system. More than once, I fell on my face, but always got up, dusted myself off, and continued on with life. I truly believed God had a better plan for me, even if I didn't understand what it was, in that present moment. I remembered, "and this too shall pass." Fortunately for me, a lot of the guidance I found was in that invisible "trunk" my mom left me.

Chapter 16

I HAD BEEN IN UTAH for several months and hadn't met many people who shared the same spiritual ideas I had. I hadn't gone to church since I moved here and that was usually a part of my weekly schedule. Even when I went on vacation, I visited whatever church was close. It didn't matter the religion, so much, as connecting with God and spiritual beings. I visited several Caribbean islands and each had their own religion and type of church service and I asked if I could join in and was graciously welcomed every time. I left each particular service feeling inspired and in awe because no matter what religion, there was always the connection and belief that we are, all "one" with God.

I was free on weekends to find a church to attend. I wanted to shop around and find the one that fit me. I glanced at my horoscope, which said, "You are moving into a much more prominent position and your emotional state will greatly improve. This person coming into your life will change it both personally and professionally and may be the unexpected catalyst to brighten your days." That sounded good, but what did it mean? Maybe a new job, or a new beau? The idea of finding a guy at church was exciting.

I've had relationships and many friends and companions, but never found that one special kindred spirit or equal partner. The one to walk side by by side on a similar spiritual path, sharing and growing together, that one who is a "keeper."

I looked forward to going to this new church. It was quite a distance from my house, and I liked the new unexplored city. I was raised in a church where the preacher's message was about being afraid of God and you could be struck down at any time and sent straight to hell. I wondered how we could be afraid of a God who gave us so much. I think heaven or hell, *is* life now, as we live it.

I was welcomed immediately and mingled to get the feel of the church and congregation. The minister gave a wonderful message, without Bible slamming and guilt rendering. They sang the most joyous songs with delightful music. The people hugged each other or shook hands and there was a social time after the service. I was excited to meet new friends and like-minded people.

I sat down between two men and was asked, "Are you new here, or from another Unity church?" and "What brought you here?"

The other guy asked, "Are you single?"

Wow, he cut right to the chase!

I answered, "Brand-new and drawn here for my spiritual health and single (thanks for asking!)."

I liked these guys right away; they were in charge of the singles group activities and we had quite the fun over the years. We held hands as we prayed and sang the Lord's Prayer. I "felt" the presence of a very interesting kindred spirit. I scanned the room, but couldn't tell where it was coming from.

I have met guys who I was attracted to and felt a connection, as if I knew them all my life and wished we could have become close, intimate friends. I would have liked to share and compare notes of our life's journey. But we would be so guarded because of something that hurt us ages ago that it felt more like ships passing in the night, not spiritual beings lending inspiration to each other. That programmed feeling to protect and hide our heart in a bucket is totally useless. We separate ourselves, we stay alone and forget, we are here to love and connect with each other. Sometimes this path is very lonely.

Sammie, Mary's friend, came over and we went out to do errands. We had both been busy and hadn't seen much of each other lately. He took me to a great bookstore where something was going on all the time.

I was routinely surprised how he always showed up when I was looking for something. I found one of my favorite author's latest books that I had been hunting for. That was a funny thing, I felt he had a new book out, but I hadn't heard any mention of it anywhere and would ask, but didn't know the title. I found poetry readings, metaphysical and spiritual classes and various church information. So this was a day of finding things.

Sammie declared, "This city needs you, you have so much to offer and share." That took me by surprise. He continued, "I want to call you a lot of the time, but I don't want to call only when I'm lonely."

"That's silly, if you called when you were in the mood, then we both wouldn't be lonely."

It was like a transfusion whenever we spent the day together. He loved my spirit and couldn't get over my positive attitude and abundance of energy, and I appreciated his worldly and spiritual knowledge, and we bounced ideas and philosophies off each other on a regular basis.

He took me to cultural events, lectures, dances, and to different churches, so I could meet people. I think that's how he met Mary was at a dance. He was a great dancer. He was a little too old for me romantically and I was a little too young for him energetically! But I always enjoyed his company. It was nice to have a friend to hang out with, to be free to laugh with and talk to, or watch movies with. Friends are a tremendous gift.

We went to hear a lady speak who had been in a small airplane crash and serious fire and had an amazing story to share. I admired the courage it took to tell the story. Her body had been severely burned. I listened to every word and felt such compassion for her and my eyes misted up as she spoke.

I hoped to meet her after the talk, but didn't think it was likely and we didn't have time to mill through the crowds afterward, where she was planning to talk with people personally. I was going to the restroom before heading home and would meet up with my friends at the front door. I looked up and she was walking toward me, as I stood alone in the aisle. Oh good, I could thank her for sharing this incredible and inspiring story. We smiled at each other and I reached out to shake her hand.

Then the strangest thing happened. As I held her hand, I "felt" the whole accident. I felt the plane, as it hit the mountain and cart wheeled on its wings until it slammed to a stop. I felt the fear and death and fire in the plane. It was as if I was in the plane with them, but not feeling the actual physical pain, only the experience.

It was so vivid, I couldn't talk and tears began to run down my cheeks. All I could do was hug her.

I had no words and it seemed like a "remembering" of something. My friends were watching this, and I couldn't even begin to explain what happened. I sat reflectively in the back seat as we drive home. What an eerie feeling. This was definitely not in my comfort zone, but I wasn't afraid either. Hmm?

I had felt energy many times before, but lately, this seemed to be more of a reoccurring thing. You know how you feel, once in a while, like someone is watching you, or as if someone is in the same room and you look around, just in case, and no one is there?

My boyfriend's employer had a Christmas party, and I was invited also. I recognized most of the people by face, but not personally and we were exchanging pleasantries. We were getting settled in for dinner and waiting for one of the ladies to return from her phone call. Just then, I had this "flash" of a message that made absolutely no sense to me.

I leaned over to the lady sitting next to me and said, "I know this sounds strange, but your grandma said to tell you, she is happy and she is okay."

She wasn't bewildered but knew exactly what I meant.

Her mom was the one who was called away from the table and returned with the news. "Your grandma just died."

The daughter told me before they left to attend to the situation that her grandma had been ill and told her, "When I die, I'll send you a message and you won't be sad because I am happy and I am okay." Then, it was me who was astounded because I never knew the lady, but got her message to pass on.

I was involved with the church's prayer ministry and on Valentine's Day we made little gifts to deliver to shut-ins. Some happened to live in frightening neighborhoods and my friend's husband was worried for us to be doing this. I had no sense of danger at all. I think we need to be aware of danger and not take unnecessary risks, but also, we create it and take it along with us…or not. We passed by houses with lots of graffiti, and scary-looking people were lurking about. I could see my friend was very uneasy.

There was a gangster-looking teen walking down the street, coming toward us, and he was wearing a tough attitude.

I told my friend, "I'll be right back."

She eased back toward her car and said in a fearful voice, "What are you doing?"

I walked toward this kid, and he had his defenses up and was ready to do whatever he felt he needed to do. I was in his environment now and he had the power.

I handed him one of the gifts, filled with candy and a wonderful affirmation about his joyous smile. He hesitantly took the small package and looked back at me suspiciously as he opened it. A broad smile covered his face. My friend almost passed out from shock as she watched him walk away, a little taller and prouder, as that "gang" attitude disappeared.

Seeing his bright smile reminded me of another story. I was quite the tomboy when I was younger and raised in a neighborhood filled with boys and only a couple of girls. I had a huge gap between my very big front teeth. I could spit between my teeth further than the boys and won all their marbles when we had a spitting contest. I could also run faster and most times, even play marbles better.

I was self-conscious of my huge teeth and what felt like a prominent overbite. I wanted braces more than anything in the world. But I also knew that wasn't even a possibility. I smiled a lot and was given silly nicknames, like "bubbles" because I was bubbling over with joy and laughter. People noticed my cheery face and warm, friendly smile. But all I saw was my big, ugly teeth. They really weren't crooked or ugly, but I thought the gap was enormous.

I went to a nursing home on a regular basis to say hi to the residents and one lady who was ninety-six, would light up when I walked in to visit.

She patted my face and exclaimed, "You are my own bright sunflower."

So I had a conversation with the man upstairs, the big dentist in the sky. I prayed, "I enjoy sharing a cheery smile and it uplifts my spirits, please fix my teeth." I now have nice, straight teeth and there is no gap and when I ran into my childhood friend, she was surprised.

"Really, you never had braces? Let me see your teeth again!"

I was fine with giving up the spitting champ title. When it was obvious Jeni inherited my horrible teeth, her mouth was immediately furnished with braces. I am so grateful every time someone compliments my smile, and I must have thanked the tooth fairy a zillion times!

I was talking about prayer with a friend, and he asked, "Does prayer really work?"

"Absolutely," I answered.

"Does God only hear you when you fall down on your knees or go to church?"

"No, he listens all day long."

He continued, "How do you pray, now that you are out of work?"

Actually, I pray just about the same. I pray with an attitude of gratitude. I don't pray in a begging or bargaining sort of way. I just talk to God. When I go for an interview, I know that God knows I need a job, and He knows my financial situation. I have faith that the right and perfect job will show up, whether it's digging up peanuts, or working for a millionaire. I believe wherever I am in any given moment is where I'm supposed to be.

There is no good, bad, or indifferent—it just *is*.

I give thanks for guidance to be qualified, or trainable, for whatever the position is, and not just spinning my wheels, as time is of the essence now.

I say thanks for helping me say the right things to convey who I am and with full assurance, what my skills are and how I can benefit their company. I am grateful for strength, patience and wisdom in these interviews and with the *knowing*, I will be hired soon on a job, for my highest good. And I end with, Thank you, God."

I was happily making a lot of new friends and experiencing the most amazing things while going to this church. Gandhi's grandson, Arun, came as a guest speaker. He talked about the "Season of Nonviolence," and planted a tree for peace, near the Peace Gardens in Salt Lake. It was a significant space where you could stroll through the serene park and travel the walkway to other lands. He and his wife radiated such peace and love, and as he spoke, you would swear his grandfather was standing right there. This incredible loving energy was just hanging in the air. It was a goose bumps moment.

People were looking around and I heard them saying, "Do you feel *that*?"

Another one replied, "I *do* feel that, it felt like a big, warm hug. My soul is overflowing and I *do* want peace everywhere, in my lifetime."

I loved when the Tibetan monks came and the church hosted several events. They shared their beautiful crafts and amazing mandala. They had an area for people to create their own mandala, as well. They were so cordial and loving and I was taking lots of pictures and probably becoming a nuisance.

The one who spoke English, teased me. "I hope you have a day job!"

I was greatly inspired when the Dali Lama came to town and I was blessed to hear him speak. The tickets were free and on a first come basis. I heard about it after it was too late to get tickets. I just knew I would be there in the audience, but didn't know how. Then, my roommate had ordered tickets early and had an extra one and slid it under my door.

I went early and waited in the long line outside, to get in ahead of the huge crowd that was gathering. I hoped I wouldn't be sitting too far back, in the auditorium.

The line was stretched down the block and I spotted several of my friends in line also. I heard beforehand there would be heavy security, so I didn't carry anything in, except my car keys, and I got in fast. I went to find a seat right away, since there were no saving seats allowed. I couldn't believe it, I was right up front. He was an amazing, humble and awe-inspiring spirit. He had a wonderful message and funny sense of humor. He's truly one of my favorites!

My friends were way in the back and waved when they saw me and asked later. "How did you get up there?

"Must be divine intervention, I guess, it just always happens!"

I was on the prayer ministry team at church and we were called to pray with people or make hospital visits. We took turns and I was out of town for a few days, and advised the church. But when I got home there was an old message that someone was having brain surgery and needed prayer. I assumed someone from the church had been with her already because someone was always available, and this message was a few days old.

I called the relative to check on her and no one had been there yet. I thought, that's unusual, hmmm, maybe I was the one who was supposed to go in the first place?

I called her at the hospital, "Do you still want someone to come and pray with you?"

"Yes, but come right away!" she answered.

"I just got back in to town and have to run by my office first."

Her urgency worried me, and I hurried to get there as soon as possible.

I introduced myself and she started talking. She had a shaved head after cancer surgery and was very depressed and feeling very unattractive. The family and the doctors expected her to die shortly. I didn't have a chance to pray with her because we continued to talk about other things. She was upset about being bald.

"Your hair will grow back soon, and in the meantime, wear a wig! The wigs that are out now are fabulous."

I noticed she was reading a book about cancer, and apparently, she thought I had cancer and survived and that's the reason she was talking to me.

I replied, "No, I have never had cancer."

Then she abruptly stated, "Thank you, goodbye."

I was dismissed. I didn't know what to think. I left there filled with questions. Why did I get this message? Everyone knew I was out of town. Why didn't anyone else visit her? What made her think

I had cancer? Why was I excused? There had to be something I was supposed to tell her. Some reason *I* needed to see her, but what was it?

I had a chat with God, "I don't understand, all these messages seem to be directed to me, what am I supposed to do or say?"

I had a sense of, "Go back tomorrow morning, on your way to work."

I tried to think of what to say, as I drove back over, and she probably wouldn't be receptive to seeing me again. I walked in her room and gave her a big smile. She was puzzled I came back, since she had dismissed me. I still had no idea of what I would say, but I knew I would be guided, when I opened my mouth.

I walked to her bedside, leaned over and took her hands and looked directly into her eyes.

"I know you think this is huge, but you are going to be *okay*, with this."

She was silent but "knew" what I said was true. Yes, she probably would die, but she would be okay.

I was in church that Sunday and saw her daughter sitting a couple of rows from me.

I inquired, "How is your mom?"

She smiled and pointed to her right. There was her mom, looking like a million bucks and wearing a lovely wig and a big smile. She made her transition several months later, but something changed that day at the hospital, it gave her the "freedom" to live.

I participated in the "World Peace Celebration." That is where people in about sixty-five countries gather at the same time, according to their time zones and noon Greenwich Mean Time, to pray and meditate for world peace. People from every religion, culture, financial status and neighborhood came together with one intention. They gathered on New Year's Eve morning for fifteen years at 5:00 AM in Utah, to create the foundation for peace in our future.

I hung up these beautiful posters everywhere and I told everyone. I went to the major TV station and asked if I could hang up the poster in their parking garage entrance. I had to have special permission for that request, so I wandered down the hall, as employees pointed to "Mr. So and So's" office.

A lady who worked in a different area of the building happened to be in the hall and smiled and asked, "What have you got there?"

I proudly showed off the finely designed piece of art.

"I want to hang this poster up, but was told to speak to the person in charge," I explained.

She said, "Wait right here." She took the poster with her and returned shortly. "Do you want to be on the local community show, *Our Town*, to announce this?"

Wow, free TV time—you bet! I would have never thought about asking for that.

Then, the next year that major news channel filmed us, live at 5:00 a.m. that is. How cool was that? Some participants wore their "Season for Nonviolence" T-shirts. The shirt displayed eight separate drawings and each with similar scenes, while changing a gun into a dove. What incredible insight.

I was in charge of the ecumenical prayer for the "Week Without Violence" ceremony at the state capitol. It's funny how these events turn up for me. I don't belong to groups and causes, but someone hears about my ability to organize or lead and they ask if I can help out. I have been invited to many functions that have changed my life.

I asked Irene, a friend of mine who was recently ordained, if she would like to say the prayer. She hadn't spoken in public often and this cause was right up her alley and she agreed.

It was a nice gathering and the media was there to cover the event. I was running late that evening and then got stuck in traffic. Since I had the prayer covered, I didn't worry. I hoped to be there to hear it first hand, but I could see my friend on the news later.

Just as I arrived at the capitol building, I heard a very unique John Denver song on the radio. That particular song held special memories for me and it brought tears to my eyes. I wondered how that song happened to be playing, at the exact time, as everyone was praying for peace?

I "felt" the power of Irene's beautiful prayer, as I left the building. Just then, in the exact place where I heard the John Denver song, I "felt" Irene's son, who had died in a car accident, when he was young.

He was relaying a message to his mother, "I am so proud of you, Mom."

I shared that with her and she was very happy.

We all search for answers, and maybe wonder who the real "Enlightened One" is. You might say it's Jesus, the Dalai Lama, Gandhi, or Buddha. But I discovered it's actually, Popeye. He always knew, "I yam, who I yam!"

Chapter 17

I WROTE IN MY JOURNAL; I love the piano, I love rainbows, I love laughter, I love flowers, I love smiles, I love lighthouses, I love kittens, and I love my children...and especially, I love surprises on the horizon!

It was Easter when I started at the new church, and I went shopping for a new outfit. I thought of Leota, even with her nasty attitude toward me, she always dressed me well. When I went to live with them, I had a broken arm and Hymie called the doctor and asked if he could cut my cast off a week early, so I could wear my beautiful new Christmas dress and white gloves. (I added to my journal, and I also love hats and gloves!) I had a marvelous hat and fancy socks and new shoes. I love all that frilly stuff, not every day, but on special occasions.

My cast had been on for an eternity already. I was playing on the monkey bars and was very good at it and started skipping one bar, then two, then I went backward, and then I fell off. When I was done crying and checked out by the school nurse, nothing appeared broken, and I was fine from the fall. Then, that next week my wrist swelled like a baseball and I had to go to the hospital and have it re-broken.

I was in a room with a little kid who chased behind a slow moving donut truck and got his hands caught in the bumper, and the truck dragged him down the street. Yikes! It pealed the skin off his legs and he was all bandaged up. I felt bad for him and couldn't believe that happened, and even with his serious injuries, he was always cheerful. But soon, he became as annoying as gum on a shoe, when he kept throwing his toys into my bed, to wake me up and play with him.

Memories poured through my head. When I turned eighteen and was finally free to move out, Hymie and Leota got a divorce, that next week. Shortly after my wedding three years later, Leota ran into her ex-husband, Jack, and they were remarried. They had married just out of high school and it lasted about a year. Leota was full of wild oats, probably her whole life.

Jack was married to his second wife for many years, until she died. He had privately loved Leota all that time, and when he ran into her thirty years later, he loved her still. He was a wonderful, kind man and she treated him so badly. He deserved better.

He gave her anything she wanted and she complained about everything. They lived out of state, which I especially liked, since it got her out of my hair!

I took the kids to visit them in Texas on holidays, and Jack always made time for them. Then, out of the blue, she started visiting us. Jack usually stayed at home because she wanted to visit her friends, and no telling what they would be doing. He thought she was staying with me. She never let me know ahead of time when she was coming, so I could plan some family time with her. I was the last on her visiting list and usually got the call that she was *in* town, only when she needed a ride back to the airport, to go home.

I always wanted some kind of recognition from her and no matter what I did or accomplished, she rarely acknowledged it. I was the only one at my high school graduation, who didn't have any parents there to witness my special event. I wondered where everyone, or any one, was. I drove home before the senior party got started, to see what could possibly have happened to them. They said they went to the graduation. How could they have been there and then not congratulated me, like the other parents? I found that hard to believe. There was no fanfare at all and that ruined my senior party plans. They said they were tired and went to bed. I spent my graduation alone.

Leota had a son, Bobby Don, with her second husband Ray, who was raised by her mother, Wyletta. He was about fifteen years older than I was and had a wife and three children. When I met him for the first time, he was drinking a cup of soda and offered me a sip. I sure didn't want this stranger's germs and turned the cup around to drink from the other side. I handed it back and noticed he was left-handed and I drank from the same side. Oh no, cooties!

When I first met Hymie's mom who lived in Texas, he told me to go up to her door, by myself, and ask for my grandma.

The cute older lady was puzzled, "I think you have the wrong house. What is your grandma's name?"

I shyly responded, "It is Granny Jones." Then she knew immediately who I was, grabbed me up in her arms, and gave me a big hug. "Come in, come in."

She was a very sweet lady and always wanted Hymie to have children, so she was very happy with me! My parents thought it was the funniest joke to play on this little old lady. I wasn't fond of their sense of humor, especially meeting all these new relatives.

I made my own way, even raising my children as a single parent, when times were really hard. I felt the only thing that Leota liked about me was my son, Alan. She adored him. She offered to baby sit for me, while I worked nights and charged me for it, but at least gave me a small discount. Wyletta lived with her then and she liked having a little tot in the house. I use to visit her in Texas during the summer.

Alan was crazy about his "Granny." It seemed like she was closer to him than Bobby Don's children, and that surprised me. It seemed our only bond was Alan. He would spend time with them during the summer and Jack gave him jobs on the farm and Alan loved them both. My son seemed to bridge our gap and Jack liked seeing her happy.

Jack would say, "Why don't you move back here, you could get a small farm and have horses and chickens and an easier life." Maybe someday, I'll give up the city life.

Later on, Leota's friends told me, "Your mom bragged on you and said you were a good mother and always told us what you were doing in California and she was proud of you." What a shocker! Would it have killed her to tell *me* that?

I got a call from Jack, "Your mom is in the hospital, she had a brain aneurysm. She was driving her car and smoking a cigarette and started to cough real hard." He paused, "The blood vessel burst in her head and they are doing brain surgery soon."

She had always smoked like a chimney, and I sort of expected something like that eventually.

He said, "You better come now, she might not survive the surgery."

I was on the next plane out. I got there and her family was gathered around. She had two twin sisters, Ouida and Frieda. The only person who wasn't there was Bobby Don. He expected her to die and didn't want to make two trips across Texas. He lived in San Antonio, and they lived near Lubbock.

She survived the surgery, and I went into her room and saw her shaved and bandaged head. A smile came to her face. She knew immediately, I would give her the "smoking" lecture. When I was a teenager we traveled back to visit Wyletta, and her husband burned up their mobile home, as well as himself. He was smoking and fell asleep in the chair. A bad combination, I would think. She fell asleep once and caught her bed on fire and was lighting up, as she threw her mattress out the door. What part of smoking in bed didn't she understand? At least she stopped that part of the bad habit. She invited me to smoke. No, thank you, I learned my lesson early on!

Leota told the nurses, "My daughter will be staying in the room with me."

They scrambled to set up a cot by her side. I had absolutely no intention of spending the night in her room, but there I was. She didn't want anyone else. Jack, her family, and friends agreed I was the one that should be with her. What were they thinking?

I had reservations about that choice of me staying overnight in her room. But to my surprise, we talked all night like we were friends at a slumber party. She asked for a cigarette, and since she just had brain surgery, I told her she just had one, maybe she wouldn't remember. After a while she caught on. They let her smoke since she probably would die anyway. She didn't die, and I flew back home after a few days.

The same remarkable thing happened when my dad had prostate surgery and was in intensive care. The whole family was there;

my sister flew in, and they all waited for him to die. They took turns visiting during the day and by the time I got there, visiting hours were over and it was time for everyone to leave.

I popped in for a brief visit and said, "I'll be back in the morning."

The nurse came in and noticed a difference in my dad's condition, and as she walked out, she smiled at me and closed the glass door behind her. I was the only one allowed to spend the night in his room. And he didn't die.

Well, Leota had another aneurysm, and I went back again. Then, she had a gall bladder attack, and even after three life-threatening surgeries, she still hung on. I was back and forth every couple of weeks, flying or driving, to visit or wait through another surgery. She did that for about four months.

Sometimes when I was there, she would be out of her head and tried to climb over the bed rails. She had this crazed look and super strength and it was very unnerving. She took *me*, on every one of her "out-of-body" journeys. She clearly described every location and event and I could visually imagine where we were. She went to Mexico and foreign places and old neighborhoods. I was the only one who could calm her down and bring her back.

That ordeal was very uncomfortable for me. When she was back, she knew her time was short and she was going to "unload" everything.

She acknowledged, "I love you so much and I was always proud of you. I'm sorry how I treated you. I was jealous because Hymie always paid attention to you and ignored me, and you always took his side." She continued, "I was angry at you when you moved away with Alan and lived by his other grandma."

I was overwhelmed with emotion and asked, "Why didn't you say anything? If you told me that I would have moved back so fast. I wasn't trying to take Alan away from you, but to make a better life for my child and I had no idea how you felt."

She held my hand and started to cry, "I'm so sorry, I made your life awful. Please forgive me."

I was stunned and it felt like a big weight was lifted, "It's all history, and now we won't be angry at each other anymore. I added the words I hadn't spoken very often, "I love you, Mom."

Then, she was at peace, probably for the first time in her life.

Wow! It felt like I was set free, I was given permission to forgive and release years of anger, sadness, and disappointment. I felt loved by her for the first time. I felt like my *junk in the trunk* was almost empty. What an emotional experience.

What was especially amazing, to me, was it felt as if my dad was saying similar words, and I could start forgiving him, at the same time, and that's when my dad and I became friends.

Bobby Don finally came to visit her almost five months later, and only after he figured she wasn't going to die, and maybe, it was rude that he hadn't visited his mother. Leota died the next day. And yes, he did have to make two trips across Texas. His wife's only concern was, she couldn't wait to get her hands on his mom's new Cadillac.

That's all she was waiting for, for Bobby Don to step up and be a good son, since he had proven otherwise, many times over the years. She was constantly bailing him out of some mess.

This was a true blessing for me because I would have really missed out on some very important lessons about love and forgiveness.

I stood next to Jack at her funeral and listened as he talked to her.

He patted her arm and said, "I will be right behind you." And he was.

Bobby Don was depressed by his mom's death and he died a couple of years later in a weird accident. He was in a truck and the door was stuck and he pushed it with his shoulder to get out and it opened abruptly and he fell out, on his head, and broke his neck.

After all three deaths, I was no longer included as their family member. Not one of her relatives ever talked to me again or answered my Christmas cards. It seemed like my whole life, I just got to "borrow" a family but never got to keep one.

I never discussed my mom's financial situation because I didn't believe it concerned me. Jack was well off, and after she died, Jack stated, "I changed our will and I want you to read them both."

He left their large house on four acres of land, most of the furniture and lots of money in a brown paper lunch bag to one of Bobby Don's daughters. She went over every day to look in on them and continued after Leota died, while the other relatives acted like vultures and ransacked all her valuable jewelry. Jack couldn't believe it.

Bobby Don's wife was angry, "They had *three* grandchildren and the other two didn't get anything." (She didn't include my children as grandchildren.)

Jack didn't have children of his own, and it was beyond belief that I was even mentioned in both wills. He was technically my stepdad, and I always thought he was a wonderful man, and the perfect grandpa. But I only knew him from a distance and not being raised by him. I enjoyed visiting them. He was my kid's grandpa and they loved him.

I never asked him for anything, over the years, even when I was struggling, I was too proud, or maybe too scared, to ask my mom to help me.

He stated, "I am as proud of you, as if you were my own daughter."

I thought how kind of him to feel that way, and tears started to roll down my cheeks.

"You have always taken care of your family and made an honest living. I have already taken care of my stepgrandson and other relatives, over the years, and now, the rest is for *you*."

Oh my god, pinch me!

Chapter 18

I WAS GOING TO CHURCH regularly and enjoyed everything about it. There were activities going on all the time and that Sunday there was a potluck barbecue after church at the local park. It felt like home, for the time being. It allowed me to continue on my spiritual path with like-minded folks.

The services were inspiring and the meditations were powerful. I saw a lot of familiar faces with big, welcoming smiles.

A lady was telling me about Jeff and said, "He's single," and gave me a wink.

Some days I'm very magnetic and can't walk quietly into a room without being noticed, or like my friend stated, "Patty, incognito? Isn't that an oxymoron?"

And on other days, I'm totally invisible. But that day, I couldn't get a guy's attention if I ran over him with my car.

When I met Jeff, it felt like an immediate connection, but he didn't notice me that day. It was a strange thing, as if he was uncomfortable and tried not to talk intimately with me but, at the same time, drawn to me. We had long eye contact, and it felt like a whole conversation was taking place in one long glance. I didn't know what to think and wondered if he was the one whose energy I felt all around me? I clearly felt that someone was there, and knew I was supposed to meet up with him at that time in my life, for whatever the pre-arranged reason was.

I signed up for one of the weekly workshops. A lady asked the minister, who was facilitating the class, "With all these positive thoughts and beliefs, why do bad things happen to good people? If we can choose, why do we choose negative things?"

Someone else asked, "How do we stay on our spiritual path, especially on bad days?"

He answered, "Love, we are here to learn love, we have to decide and follow what is true. We have to continue to strive for love, no matter what. We need to believe in God and have faith and trust there is a divine plan, for all of us."

He shared a book he was reading about groups of souls and their journey that would help us better understand the bigger picture. I couldn't wait to read it.

I believe in reincarnation and that souls do come back in groups in the same lifetime. I feel we do have a prearranged divine plan, that we have chosen, and it covers many of this life's issues. We meet up with these souls, somewhere on our journey for unfinished business, karma, relationships, illness, healing, guidance, or inspiration, etc. Sometimes it's just to remind us of who we are, and why we are here. I think Leota, Jack and Bobby Don were in a group of souls and their work here was done, they had made that connection, or reconnection, interacted for whatever the purpose was and then the group was free to leave.

They always say, "Death comes in threes."

It's like when you're running late and rushing to get where you're going and traffic is at a standstill and everyone has their "bad mood" hat on, and you're thinking about the meeting or the kids and what's for dinner. Then, that one person looks over at you from the next car and smiles, and in that moment you "know" that you know that person, not by name, but by their familiar spirit. And if by magic, amidst the chaos of the day, you feel calm, but also filled with gratitude, for the reminder.

You may never see that person again, that one soul, who stopped by at that precise moment, to lift your spirits or just say "hi," or "it's okay," and your whole attitude changes. What a unique connection.

We stood in a circle and held hands after the meditation. We sang a beautiful song that created an amazing bond to connect us all. The facilitator said the perfect words that made us feel as if God was talking directly to each one of us. He asked, "Who are you?" and paused, "Now listen for the answer."

I had my eyes closed as I pondered his question. I heard my inner voice, "You are light, you are love, you are a rainbow."

I left there feeling uplifted, but then very lonely. I didn't have anyone to share my inspiring evening with. I wished I had someone to talk to that night, or the bigger wish, for a partner to go to the classes with me. I stopped at the convenience store before I went home and saw a guy wearing the weirdest, ugliest shorts I've ever seen. It looked like he just stepped out of a seventies red plaid, shag carpet. A smile came to my face, and any thoughts of loneliness quickly evaporated, as I held back every ounce of laughter that was close to breaking free.

He was next to me at the counter and looked over and said, "You have a great smile!" If I had to guess, I would say this guy was one of those kindred spirits who popped in, when I needed to lighten up because no one could possibly own shorts like *that*!

I met a fellow named Barry and kept calling him Bob. It was as if I knew him before, but his name wasn't Barry then. Did I recognize his soul from some other life? I think we do remember people from previous lives and now, this life, their roles are different, but we still remember, or judge, them as they were, and don't give them the chance to be who they are now.

One day I was lying on my bed and trying to figure out an answer to a difficult situation. I "felt" a presence in my room. It felt like a joyful little angel, popping in to give me support for my trying day. The message made me smile. I wondered who that cheerful spirit was.

Then I felt this sweet little energy lean over my shoulder and look up into my face and giggle, "You know who I am."

So we hang on to crummy things or bad relationships or old hurts and angers that don't serve our highest purpose any longer because it's what we know, it fits like an old shoe. Even if that shoe gives us blisters, we wear it anyway.

One minister shared many inspiring messages with the congregation, and I liked the story of the bird that slammed into the window time and time again, trying to get out. The door was only a short distance away and it was open. But the bird did what it knew and wouldn't take any other option to find the open door to its freedom. Does that sound like humans, or what?

We talked about meditation and how effective it is and everyone had their own style and outcome. Praying is talking to God, and meditating, is listening. We did a Sufi dance at the end of the class. We formed an inner and outer circle and faced each other while touching palms and said a blessing, then bowed and changed partners. We rotated around the circle so everyone connected with, and honored, that other person. It was a delightful experience. As we went around the circle, Jeff wound up in front of me. He looked intensely into my eyes as I stared into his. It was a different feeling from anyone else. It was a sensual and gentle moment and I *did* remember this soul. But now, what are our roles?

A few times over the years, I spoke to different spiritual leaders about these unusual situations that I found myself in. I learned to listen to my inner guide and didn't question it often. But at times, I didn't understand why I got messages that didn't make any sense or involve me, so to speak.

On each occasion, they all answered, "You are *known* in the universe." Oh boy—more questions…

Chapter 19

THE KEY TO LIBERATION IS to find the path to inner peace and thereby transcend choice or result.

I was on the road and heading home through Las Vegas and felt like treating myself. I hadn't dated in a while and wanted to go places and do fun things, but felt I needed a date. I thought, what the heck, I could wait for a date and miss out on some neat things or I could take "myself" out on a date. I decided to enjoy the Sunday brunch and maybe take in a movie.

I was sitting alone at the table and enjoying my meal and several waiters passing by, stopped to talk to me. I guess they thought I was lonely. A nice couple from Indiana started talking to me and said they were expecting their first child. It was becoming comical, I was attracting everyone and it seemed they all had a story, to tell me. When I held the door open for a man, he told me all about his day.

It was a five-hour drive home from Vegas, and the time flew by as I was filled with joy from my pretend date. I wanted to be in the "date ether" again. I had been dateless, but not desperate, for some time.

I went to the meditation classes, and after lots of practice, I was able to quiet my mind and go deep down within myself, after a lot of practice. I found it was easy to meditate every day and did it first thing in the morning.

I had to get out of bed and sit in a chair or on the floor because I would fall back to sleep so fast.

The soft piano and flute music put me at peace in moments. I had several special places to drift off to, but the lighthouse was my favorite. I didn't know who played the piano in the center of the room, but the music always filled my heart when I was there.

A guy was playing the piano that day in church for our special music. I listened and tried to concentrate, but something about his playing was familiar, and that tune…where had I heard that before? All of a sudden, I remembered—that music was the one being played on the piano in my lighthouse, in my meditations. I couldn't believe my ears.

I think we should acknowledge anyone who has inspired us, by telling him or her, or maybe sending a note. It's like tithe; we should tithe to the source of our spiritual nourishment. Some say, charities don't count, you need to tithe only to a church. I think we can do both, whether tithing by time, talent or treasure.

I went up to him afterward and said, "I want to share an unusual story with you."

He listened attentively as I told him about my special lighthouse, and the piano, and he was the one playing it, as I meditated. He blinked back a couple of tears and took a breath and hugged me.

He responded, "Thank you, I've never heard that compliment before."

I said, "No, thank *you*."

Gordon was one of the first guys I met at church and I liked being included in any of his boating adventures. He gave me a big "survival" hug when he saw me. We worked on Habitat for Humanity together and what a great experience. I asked Jeni if she wanted to work on the projects with me to build homes for the homeless because it was quite rewarding. She was open to any humanitarian experience that I was involved in. I appreciated her doing that.

I read a story about hugs. It said we need several hugs a day, just to stay psychologically balanced, with a minimum of four hugs for maintenance and twelve hugs for growth. There should be an official "Hug Day," to hug everyone—hug your friends, hug your parents, hug your children, and hug the dog. Hug a tree. Blow a kiss to the fish, and send a hug to a mug!

I started volunteering for more church events and taking classes and meeting more of the type of friends I wanted in my life. I enjoyed getting out and laughing and playing more and making new friends.

Several years ago, I had a falling out with my best friend, Rene, and I wasn't interested in making another close, intimate friend. It was one of those useless "I want to be right" fights, and we never patched things up. I had a lot of friends, but very few that I shared my deepest secrets with. We shared everything and she was closer to me than a sister and I considered her family. We spent the holidays together, went on weekend outings, trudged through boyfriends, talked on the phone for days, and all that other best friend stuff.

Once we went to a baseball game and tried to smuggle in wine coolers and peanuts. We got through the gate and walked carefully down the steps, so no one would notice our contraband. Then the bag tore and we did a juggling act to save the contents. The bottles rolled down the aisles and peanuts flew into the air and were landing everywhere. We tried to leave the scene of the crime quickly, but when we looked back, our other friend was trying to pick up the peanuts. We couldn't stop laughing, as she hurried to catch up with us.

"No, Security Officer, we don't know who that peanut lady is and we can't imagine where those coolers came from."

You know it's bad when your friend talks to one of the ball players and says, "Patty said..." and he knows which Patty!

So I realized it was time to open up and invite new friends in. I bet I missed out on many good times because my heart was closed off from a previous experience that had nothing to do with the present moment. I missed my friend, Rene and I messed up bad by not making amends.

I had many male friends and was recently invited to a girl's night out and had forgotten how much fun that was. This new friend had cancer and lived her brief, but full life, sharing her delightful "mime" talent with others, and she made many people happy.

I felt lucky when she asked the new kid on the block out to play.

Chapter 20

I LIVE IN THE PRESENT. I remember the past and have faith in the future. Sometimes, the only way out is through. I now open the door to my heart and let the pure essence of unconditional love flow in and out as a sea in perpetual motion.

I was at my desk and writing about some of the workshops I attended over the years that just showed up when I needed them. I barely hit the keys that spelled out "when I needed them," and it happened again. So I have to tell you about it.

I was having an emotional day and thought I would write to take my mind off things. I was trying to hang onto any positive thoughts just to get through the day. I still believe, "And this too shall pass" and sometimes I just have to hang on and ride the ride.

When my children were young, they were enrolled in all sorts of classes and fun summer activities that taught them a variety of things and kept them busy. I absolutely loved tap and ballet, and I couldn't wait for my daughter to love them too. I bought her little tap shoes and the cutest leotards and she was adorable, as she stood lifeless in the middle of the floor. She never tapped a foot for six weeks. She liked ballet, and the recitals were fun, but tap was out. I was in awe of tap dancers. One of my friends took up tap dancing as an adult, and I was so impressed that she pursued her lifelong dream. There seemed to be magic about tap movements, and the noise of the taps took me away, to a land of enchanting dreams, like the Shirley Temple movies, where there was always a happy ending.

I turned on the TV and Oprah was on. There was a seven-year-old on her show who was an amazing little tapster. Oh, how precious. I was dazzled by his performance and this was a special treat. But wait, there's more. Then, a commercial came on advertising, *The Lord of the Dance*. I knew they were coming to town but couldn't afford to see this show. I paused for a moment to capture the feeling, as if I were going.

Just then, a wonderful fellow named Steve called. I have to tell you about him. He is an astonishingly, selfless man and probably a guardian angel to many people. His heart is so full and it seemed that we always volunteered for the same things. Every Christmas, a group from the church rented a bus and went caroling to several different shelters and children's homes.

I called ahead and got the number of adults and the ages of the kids, so if anyone wanted to take gifts to some or all, they had an idea of what was needed at each location. It seemed he lived for that time of year. He was definitely a secret Santa. He went to the store and bought bundles of new shoes and toys for all the children and I always laughed as he tried to wrap them up. Everyone got a present.

One of the children was negotiating with him for a different type of truck for next year. It was so sweet to watch him. Steve smiled brightly as he got back on the bus to go to the next home, with residents of different circumstances, but getting the same results.

His call came as a very incredible surprise. He said, "I have two tickets for (what else, but…) *The Lord of the Dance*, I can't go, do you want them?"

I asked how much they cost.

He replied, "No charge, they are a gift for you."

How could he possibly know how I felt about tap dancing? How did his call come just as I saw the ad or the little kid? Usually, I'm not even home at that time of day.

I was stunned! "Oh my gosh, yes, I'll take them." I was so grateful and kept saying "Thank you, thank you," and he was almost embarrassed since the tickets seemed trivial to him, but it meant the world to me. The seats were front and center as usual.

A while back, a friend said, "Let Patty go for the tickets, she always gets the best seats." It just cracks me up. By coincidence, something happens to the seats, and they are changed and we wind up in the front. We went to the theater to see a live performance of *The Lion King* that had been sold out. The box office called and said there was a last-minute cancellation for two tickets and did I want them. It felt like we had the best seats in the house and saw every costume and detail up close. It was awesome!

We went to see Billy Joel and the seats for our group were perfect, and there was an aisle in front of our row, so no one could block our view.

I walked up to the stage to take a picture, and a lady sitting in the second row said, "Why don't you take these two seats up here, the people had to leave."

I ran back to get my friend and we enjoyed front row seats!

Once, my husband and I were in Las Vegas and I wanted to see Andy Williams, but he had other plans and wasn't willing to pay such a high price to see him. I would have given up any of my gambling budget to hear him sing, and I just knew I was going to see him that night, but how?

Dave went to the sports area and I went to play Keno, and on the first game, I won the exact amount to buy two tickets for Andy's show and had $5 left over.

I ran to get my husband who probably hoped he was off the hook, and I exclaimed, "Look, I won at Keno, and we can go see Andy Williams."

He said, "But the game is on."

I responded impatiently, "We have to get in line now."

What is it with men? I guess sports and romance never mix? They were seating us near the back and I heard, if you tipped them, you might get a better seat. I had the five dollars, which might move us up one or two rows closer, and that was fine with me.

I handed the guy the money and he said, "Come with me."

I couldn't imagine where he was taking us. We had a table right at the stage, in the first row. Andy Williams came out and took my hand as he started to sing, and I almost had a heart attack. Best five bucks I ever spent!

Then, there was the Bobby Vinton concert when I was in high school. I was trying to look cool and wearing my beautiful head of imitation curls. They were quite fashionable then. He was coming down the aisle from the back and the spotlight followed him, and we started giggling as he came closer. Then, one of those, "Oh no, I hope I'm dead moments…"

His microphone cord caught the back of my fake hair as he passed us and my hair slid down over my face.

The bright spotlight was capturing the whole thing as if the sun just fell into the auditorium, making sure everyone saw it. I was grateful he kept walking down the aisle as he sang, and that really embarrassing moment soon disappeared, as the show continued, with us "oowing and awing" at his romantic lyrics.

I enjoy going to "hands on" workshops, taking different classes, and attending seminars on a variety of topics, some for fun and others for education or for my spiritual growth. I had a busy schedule most of the time, but I always knew which one I should attend because my calendar amazingly freed up, or the money unexpectedly turned up.

I heard about a *Management by Accountability* conference, and it was coming up soon and sounded interesting. I wanted to go, but it wasn't in that month's budget and maybe I would go next time. I scanned the brochure anyway to see who the speaker was. It was the author whose book had inspired me so many years ago, Shakti Gawain. Then, I really wished I could go. I no sooner thought that, when the phone rang.

It was my boss, "You got a bonus for that project last month and I forgot to put it on your pay check." It was the *exact* amount I needed for the conference, including travel, meals and motel expenses!

The church was putting on a weeklong conference and planning to hold it at the resort where I worked. We were looking for notable speakers who might also hold a variety of inspirational workshops. I had a list of "who's who" to work from and planned to negotiate their fees with them, as we were using this conference as a fundraiser. I was amazed when some prominent lecturers agreed to lower their fee, while others said they had a standard, nonnegotiable speaking fee. One of the names mentioned was Shakti Gawain!

The minister asked me, "Can you contact any of these people and see if they are interested in our conference?"

I responded, "I can call all these people, but by coincidence, I'm going to Shakti Gawain's conference next week and I can ask her personally."

She was happy to do it!

Coincidence, I think not!

Chapter 21

I WAS SITTING IN CHURCH and listening to the morning message and I heard my inner voice say, "What a sweet face." I was near the middle of the auditorium and had to take a second look at the minister, not that he didn't have a sweet face, but it wasn't something I would be thinking, about him.

It was Monday morning and I was getting ready for work and turned on the news and heard, "John Denver's plane went down in Monterey, California." I enjoyed his music and respected him as a person, and even though I wasn't his biggest fan, I felt sad about the news. I thought I would like to go to his memorial service, which would probably be on Friday, in Aspen.

Then I thought, or even go to Monterey and just sit on the beach and reflect on this person who had touched so many lives. I loved Monterey and went there often when I lived in California, when I just needed to "be." I instantly started making mental excuses because even the thought sounded ridiculous.

My inner self said, "Well, what's stopping you?" I snapped into immediate awareness. "Nothing is stopping me. I will follow what my heart is saying and go to Monterey."

I called my boss and said I had to go out of town for a few days. I didn't feel the need to give her too many details. I packed my car and was on the road in an hour. Maybe I would rent a plane and have an instructor take me up to do a "private" fly-by and tip a wing over the area, to express my personal thanks. I was in no hurry and loved the scenic drive down the coast. I planned to camp somewhere along the way.

It was about a fourteen-hour drive, and I listened to my John Denver CDs and embraced the glorious sunshine and sparkling lake as I entered and passed through Lake Tahoe. I got to the beach in Monterey on Tuesday afternoon and his plane went down so close to the shore, I sat right there and meditated and prayed and sent out blessings for his soul's new journey.

It was the most beautiful day.

His plane went down close to the shore

The sky was a cloudless soft blue and the ocean was calm.

They were still pulling in the wreckage and people were stopping by to pay their respects. It was the most beautiful day. The sky was a cloudless soft blue and the ocean was calm. It seemed to me, on that day, he had everything he loved, in the palm of his hand. He had

On that day, he had everything he loved, in the palm of his hand.

been golfing with friends and flying in a place he loved, his family was close, and things were looking up for him. It would sure be the thing I ordered, as a last request.

I sat on the rocks and was amazed at how calm all the sea critters were. I surveyed the area and there seemed to be a lot more sea and air animals than I remembered. Birds and little furry animals came up and sat real close to me. I was surprised because they were there voluntarily, and I wasn't offering any snacks. I observed the unusual activity and thought maybe I should take a picture because this story would sound so strange when I told anyone. I fumbled in my camera bag and the animals sat there until I snapped the shot. Hmm?

Birds and little furry animals came up and sat real close to me.

I fumbled in my camera bag and the animals just sat there until I snapped the shot.

There was a long, black limousine parked at the curb. I suspected it had something to do with John's body being cremated that day, but I didn't feel the need to inquire. I took my beach chair closer to the water and listened to his songs and watched as people came and went, while others as they passed by and heard the music, shared what that particular song meant to them. I kept thinking how "peaceful" and beautiful this day was.

Lots of sea and air animals were close by

How "peaceful" and beautiful this day was.

I planned to leave later in the day after I had my time to say goodbye. Apparently, I was lost in my own thoughts and a lady appeared. I didn't even hear her walking up.

She said, "There is going to be a memorial service for John tonight, so spread the word."

I thought a service would have been done already, but I certainly would stay for this one. I had no set schedule and could spend the night anywhere on the drive home.

I heard other's reminiscing, "What a sweet face."

The group started building a memorial on the beach

They made a large circle with small boulders and beach limbs

They laid out a huge cross of rocks in the sand

The group started building a memorial on the beach. They laid out a huge cross of rocks in the sand and made a large circle with small boulders and beach limbs and spelled out *John Denver* with seaweed, inside the circle. People were dropping off flowers and news crews were filling the beach.

They spelled out "John Denver" is seaweed, inside the circle

news crews were filling the beach.

I sat quietly and watched all the activity. I looked down the beach and the news trucks jammed the streets and parking spaces. They set up remotes everywhere.

If anyone wanted to know what was going on, I said, "They are having John's service about 6:00 p.m., right down there."

Then, a newsman walked up to me and asked, "Who is doing the service?"

I thought all the details were taken care of by the way everyone was putting this together.

I answered, "Well, the lady who told me…" and I visually scanned the beach for her, "would probably know…" But she was nowhere to be seen. I was puzzled. Where did she go? It seemed like she was the one in charge. I didn't know why he asked me that question, since I was minding my own business and not contributing anything to the memorial itself.

He stood there waiting for my response and then others gathered close to hear the answer. I looked around at all the faces and tried once more to spot that lady, and he asked me again.

"Well, who is doing the service tonight?"

I paused and took a deep breath and stated, "That would be *me*."

A couple of John's neighbor's walked by to verify the time and told me, "This service should have been on Monday."

The other neighbor pointed to me, "We couldn't, because *she* wasn't here yet." Goose bumps!

Someone else asked, "What kind of religious service are you doing?"

I liked that question, "No specific religion, but a service that John would like."

The full moon glistened in the sky and created an endless path on the water.

The full moon glistened in the sky and created an endless path on the water. The birds seemed to fly in a formation closer to the ground. All of a sudden, some playful seals were bouncing through the water like skipping stones. Everyone agreed that *had* to be John. He would have loved that! His presence illuminated the night sky.

Birds seemed to fly in a formation closer to the ground

Some playful seals were bouncing through the water like skipping stones

Everyone agreed that had to be John!

His presence illuminated the night sky.

    Dusk was approaching as his fans and neighbors gathered in a circle around the memorial and I suggested we all hold hands. I said a prayer and we sang *Amazing Grace*, as well as several of his songs and then we told "John" stories. The surrounding energy was alive.

At one point, I felt like I was out of my body and he was present and standing right there. A photographer's flash and click, click, click brought me back. Did he notice something odd also?

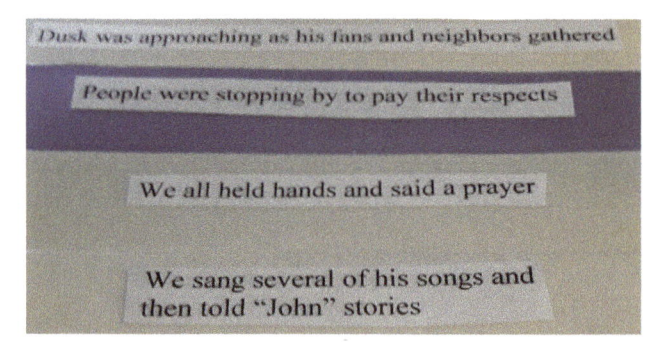

Dusk was approaching as his fans and neighbors gathered

People were stopping by to pay their respects

We all held hands and said a prayer

We sang several of his songs and then told "John" stories

John's friends and neighbor's

His friends and neighbors came up to me afterward and told me such loving stories. "Remember when Zach did... (this or that)" and "Remember how John was about planting all those trees!"

I listened and smiled, and they were quite astonished when I said, "I never met John."

Here's the eulogy I wrote:

Welcome, I am so grateful that we are gathered here on this glorious evening to pay tribute to John Denver and celebrate his life. He is an inspiration to us all.

John sang to our hearts and told us stories about real life. He made us laugh and reminded us how to love. He was there for us on good days and days of despair. He was there when we got married, had children, and faced problems. He was there when we laughed and played under the stars. He was there when we celebrated and also when we cried. John's music was always there for us.

He showed us how to *be* alive and truly live and love all of life. We all knew John through his music, which was his *highest truth*. Probably everyone here feels a personal, intimate relationship with him. We are so blessed that John chose to share his life with us.

Tonight we are here to honor John and say "thank you" and let him know how much he was deeply loved by so many people. We will have a moment of silence to reflect on John's life, love, divine spirit and especially, his sweet smile.

We will rejoice in the knowing that he is at peace and lived his life to the fullest. He shared his whole soul with all of us and in every song, every story, every muppet giggle, every snowflake, John will remain alive in our hearts.

There are many legends and superstars, there are few heroes and role models…John was all of these.

We ended by holding hands and raising them up and shouting to the sky as loud as we could, so John could hear us…

"THANK YOU, WE LOVE YOU, JOHN!"

That was the most incredible thing I've ever experienced and when the service was over, I still couldn't believe it. What just happened here? The energy in the air and on the beach were magical. It was a very special evening for so many people who needed to express what they felt. It was October 15, and I was on my way home. I wondered how John would have felt about his service. In that *very* instant, I had a "flash" of a big smile, dancing in the breeze. There was no face, but it was definitely John's smile.

I heard, "You did good, Thank you."

"Love is why I came here in the first place,
Love is now the reason I must go,
Love is all I ever hoped to find here,
Love is still the only dream I know."
(John Denver, *Seasons of the Heart*, the CD John Denver definitive all-time greatest hits are totally my favorites also!)

John Denver
December 31, 1943 - October 12, 1997

"He lived his life in a major key"
Milton Okun

"Love is why I came here in the first place,
Love is now the reason I must go,
Love is all I ever hoped to find here,
Love is still the only dream I know."
John Denver, Seasons of the Heart

JOHN DENVER MONTEREY MEMORIAL SERVICE OCTOBER 14, 1997

I did the *World Peace Celebration* for a few years and this one year I wasn't available. I asked someone else to coordinate it. I was at work and the John Denver song, "*Aspen Glow,*" came on the radio. I didn't recall ever hearing that song. Then, I hear the words, in my mind, "You have to do it." I was puzzled. Do what? Right then, the phone rang and the person in charge of the service couldn't do it. I was on short notice but did get it together, which by coincidence, the date of December 31, is John Denver's birthday!

I went back to work, after playing hooky for those few days in Monterey. My boss handed me a newspaper, and I was on the front page.

She inquired, "Is this you?"

"Yes, that would be me!"

I was wondering how to end this book and my word processor started acting up and typing strange characters and then it ran out of ribbon and broke.

But I do have one more story!

A friend from church was planning a large camping trip in the mountains and I didn't care for that specific location.

He said, "Get in the car right now and I will take you up there and you can see this spot will be perfect for our group."

I asked, "Why do you care if I like the location or not?"

He replied, "We want a big crowd to join us, and if you go, they will too, because a lot of people, ride *your* bus!"

I am still amazed as the stories continue. A favorite song of mine is, "What the World Needs Now, is *love*..." And it's still true today.

As long as we are on this planet, we are a "work in progress," and every day is a new day and another chance to be the very best we have been created to be.

Love and be kind to yourself, love and be kind to humanity, we're all we have, for now.

It's like Disneyland in the days of designated ride coupons that measured how mild or exciting each ride was, with "A", being the easiest. I suggest you take the "E" coupon ride.

LIFE IS A PARTICIPATION sport...

THE END

John's bench in Monterey CA

JOHN DENVER
THE LEGACY CONTINUES...

"What a sweet face.

Monarch Grove Butterfly Sanctuary

Arriving in October, the Monarch Butterflies cluster together on the pines and eucalyptus trees of the Sanctuary.

Monarch Butterfly Sanctuary Monterey CA

ASPEN COMMISSION COMPANY
GENERAL COMMISSION MERCHAN
STRAITON & STORM'S
OWL
DENVER
DISTRIBUTORS
CIGAR NOW 5

Lyle Lovett

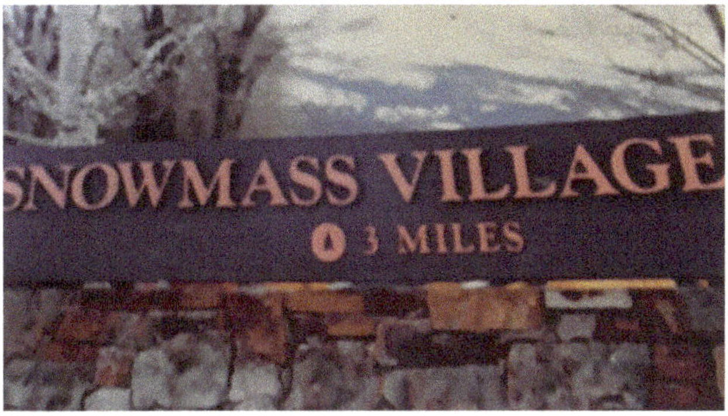
SNOWMASS VILLAGE
3 MILES

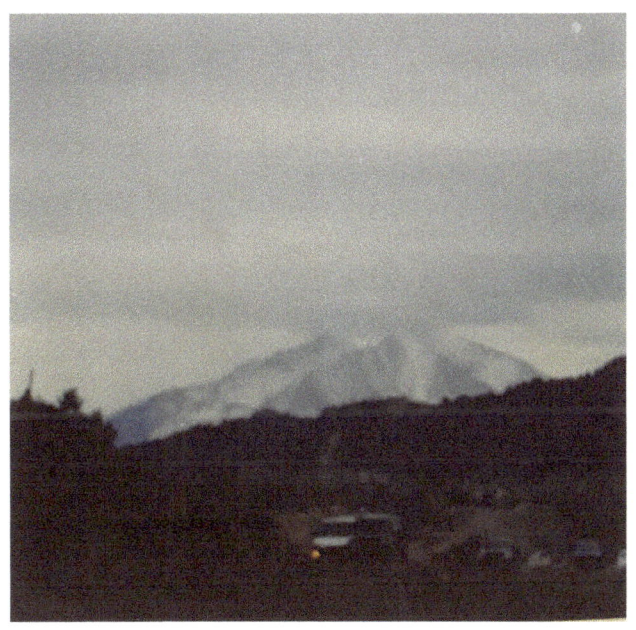

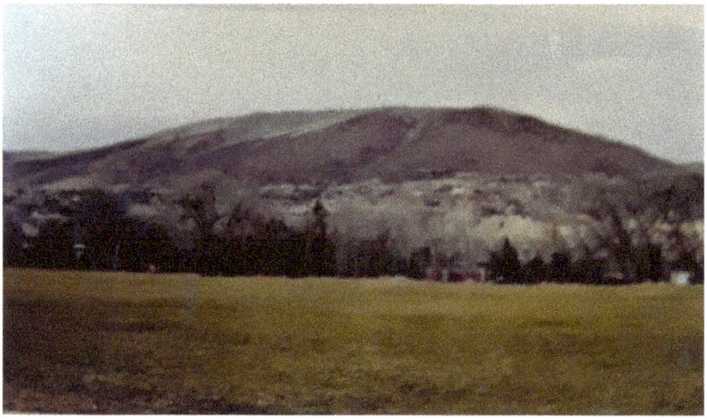

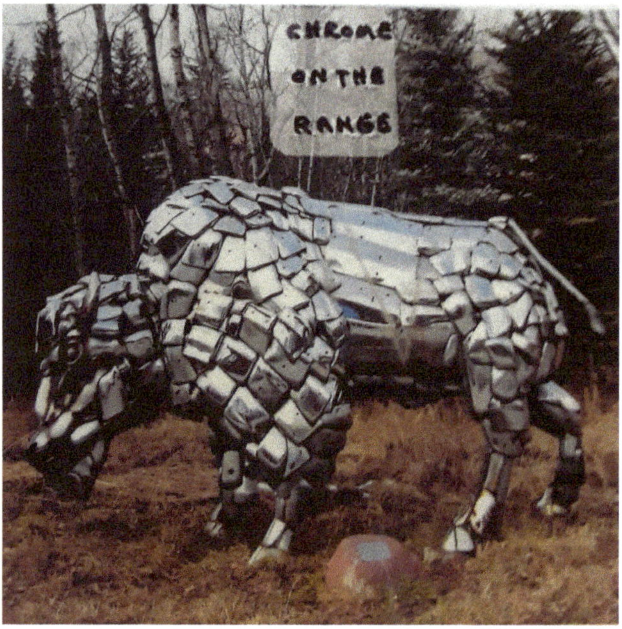
CHROME
ON THE
RANGE

Rio Grande
Trail
City of Aspen Parks & Recreation
John Denver Sanctuary
JOHN
DENVER
SANCTUARY

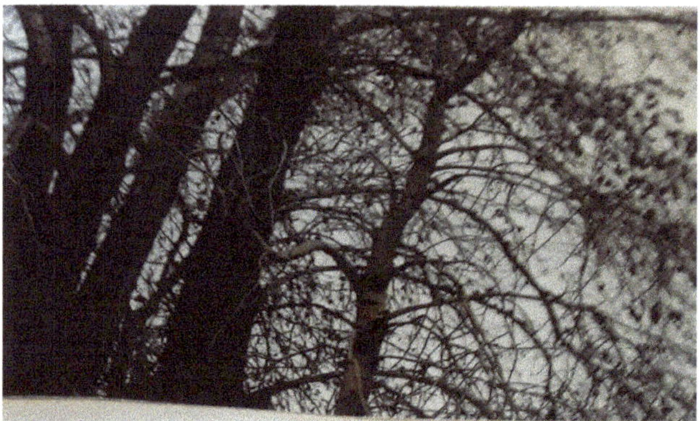

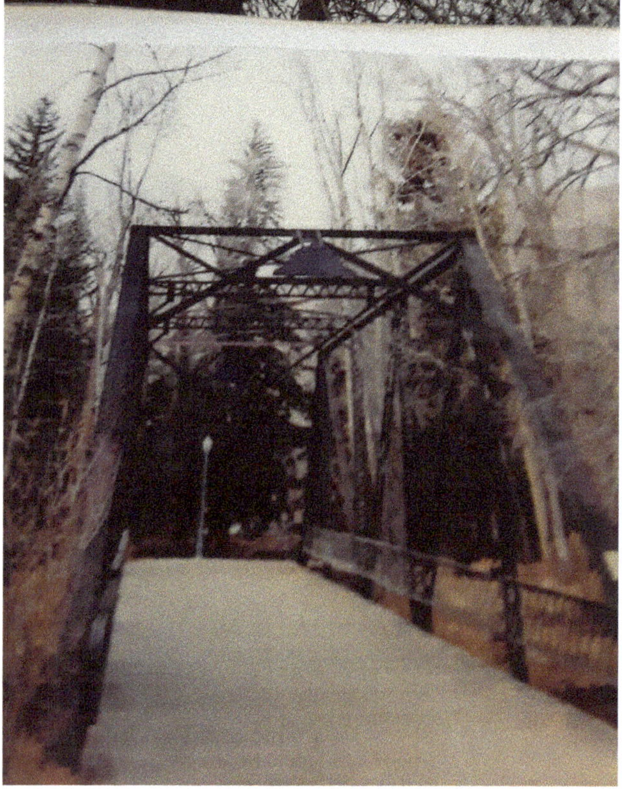

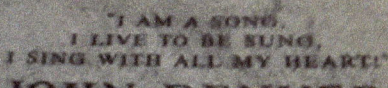

"I AM A SONG,
I LIVE TO BE SUNG,
I SING WITH ALL MY HEART!"
JOHN DENVER
COMPOSER, MUSICIAN, FATHER,
SON, BROTHER, FRIEND
DECEMBER 31, 1943 – OCTOBER 12, 1997

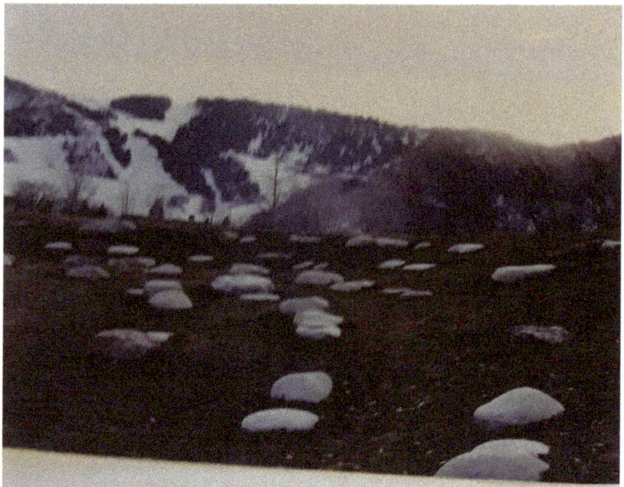

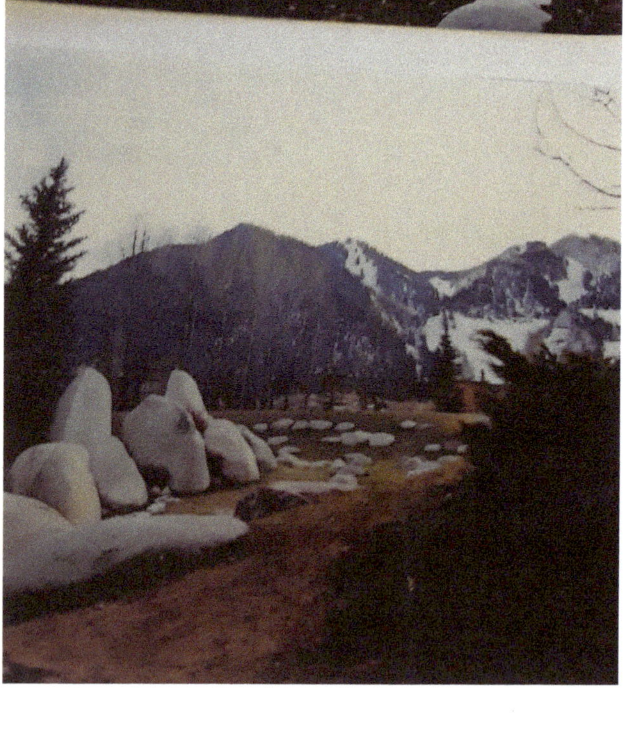

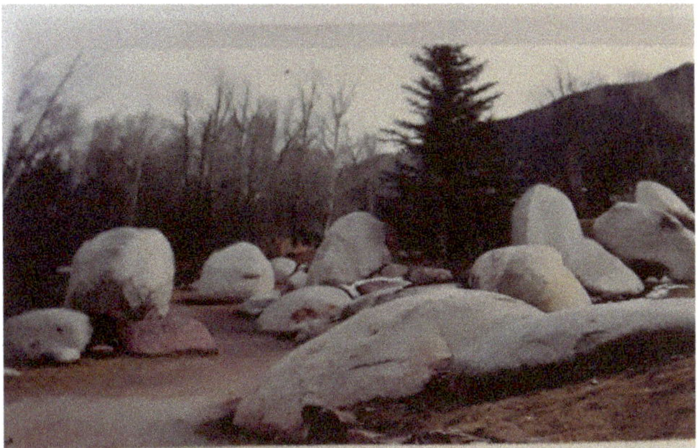

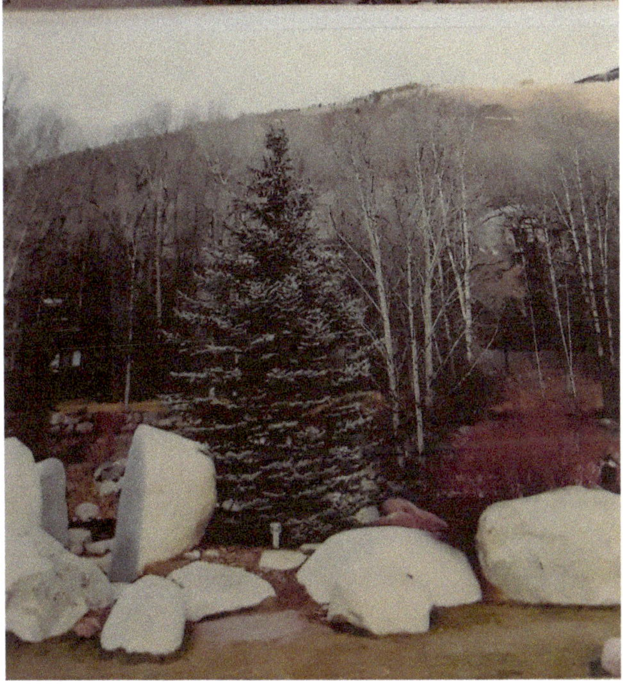

ROCKY MOUNTAIN HIGH

He was born in the summer of his twenty-seventh year
Comin' home to a place he'd never been before
He left yesterday behind him
You might say he was born again
You might say he found a key for every door

When he first came to the mountains his life was far away
On the road and hangin' by a song
But the string's already broken and he doesn't really care
It keeps changin' fast and it don't last for long

But the Colorado Rocky Mountain High
I've seen it rainin' fire in the sky
The shadow from the starlight is softer than a lullaby
Rocky Mountain High

He climbed cathedral mountains, he saw silver clou[ds]
He saw everything as far as you can see
And they say that he got crazy once and
He tried to touch the sun
And he lost a friend but kept his memory

Now he walks in quiet solitude the forest and the st[reams]
Seeking grace in every step he takes
His sight has turned inside himself to try and under[stand]
The serenity of a clear blue mountain lake

[Of] the Colorado Rocky Mountain High
[I've] seen it rainin' fire in the sky
[Talk to] him if he'd a cooler man
[to] he never saw
an eagle fly
[Colo]rado Rocky Mountain High

PERHAPS LOVE

Perhaps love is like a resting place
A shelter from the storm
It exists to give you comfort
It is there to keep you warm
And in those times of trouble
When you are most alone
The memory of love will bring you home

Perhaps love is like a window
Perhaps an open door
It invites you to come closer
It wants to show you more
And even if you lose yourself
And don't know what to do
The memory of love will see you through

Oh, love to some is like a cloud
To some as strong as steel
For some a way of living
For some a way to feel
And some say love is holding on
And some say letting go
And some say love is everything

In Commemoration of
JOHN DENVER
Henry John Deutschendorf, Jr.

Dedicated September 23, 2007
at the site of the crash of John's plane, Long Bay, 11553

"... So welcome the wind and the wisdom she joys
Follow her summons when she calls again
In your heart and your spirit let the breezes surround
Lift up your voice then and sing with the wind..."

— "Windsong" by John Denver and Joe Henry

CPSIA information can be obtained
at www.ICGtesting.com
Printed in the USA
LVHW021636251022
731517LV00012B/365